The Lion
Storyteller Christmas Book

The Lion
Storyteller
Christmas
Book

Bob Hartman

Illustrations by Susie Poole

LION
Children's Books

For Jon

Text copyright © 2000 Bob Hartman
Illustrations copyright © 2000 Susie Poole
This edition copyright © 2000 Lion Publishing

The moral rights of the author and illustrator
have been asserted

Published by
Lion Publishing plc
Sandy Lane West, Oxford, England
www.lion-publishing.co.uk
ISBN 0 7459 4071 4
Lion Publishing
4050 Lee Vance View, Colorado Springs,
CO 80918, USA
ISBN 0 7459 4071 4

First edition 2000
10 9 8 7 6 5 4 3 2 1

A catalogue record for this book is available
from the British Library

Library of Congress CIP data applied for

Typeset in 13/17 GaramdITC LtBT
Printed and bound in Spain

Contents

Introduction

Candles and stars. Trees and bells. Mangers and shepherds
and brightly wrapped presents. These are some of the things that remind us
of Christmas. I think that stories need to be added to that list as well. To my
list anyway. Because stories have always been an important part of Christmas
for me.

There were the cartoons—poor Charlie Brown trying desperately to
decorate his scrawny little tree. There were the films—particularly that old
black-and-white 'Christmas Carol' with the creepy doorknocker that always
made me hide my eyes. And then there was that other story—the one that
started it all. The one with me in my bathrobe, and my allergic brothers
sneezing in the hay, and my sister's doll masquerading as the Son of God.

When I was a child, Christmas was bursting with stories. And, for many
years as a pastor and professional storyteller, I have enjoyed the privilege
of telling Christmas stories. So, in this book, I would like to share some of
those stories with you. The story of the first Christmas for a start. Then stories
about the origins of different Christmas traditions. And, finally, a collection of
Christmas tales and legends. They are from many cultures and lands (and I've
even sneaked in one or two of my own). But each story reflects, in its own
way, the wonder and joy we associate with this most special time of year.

Whenever I write a Christmas story, I always think of it as a kind of gift
for its hearers. I work that little bit longer, imagine that little bit harder and
usually, like the best gifts, it turns out to be a pretty good surprise. That's
my hope for this book as well. That you will see these stories as a kind of gift.
A gift to you and your family, and a thank you to the one who was the first
and most surprising Christmas gift of them all.

Bob Hartman

Christmas Stories
from the Bible

*Over the centuries, the Christmas stories
in the Bible have been passed on from
generation to generation. These new
retellings capture the joy, wonder and
celebration that surrounded the birth
of a very special baby, Jesus.*

A Surprise for Zechariah

Gabriel was an angel. A very busy angel.

God decided that the time had come to send his Son into the world. So he chose Gabriel to get everything ready.

The first thing Gabriel did was to visit an old priest called Zechariah. He and his wife, Elizabeth, had no children of their own. And that made them very sad. So, one day, while Zechariah was working in the temple in Jerusalem, Gabriel appeared to him—bright and shiny, glowing and gold!

Zechariah had never seen an angel before, so he was very frightened. His legs turned to jelly. He quivered, he shivered and he shook.

'Don't be afraid,' said Gabriel gently. 'For I am here to bring you good news! You and your wife have been praying for a child, and soon your prayers will be answered. You will have a baby. You will call him John. And when he grows up, he will help the world get ready to meet God's own special Son!'

'But my wife and I are so old,' said Zechariah. 'How can we possibly have a child?'

'I'll prove it to you,' said Gabriel with a smile. 'From this very moment until the time the child is born, you will not be able to speak a word. That way you will know that what I say is true.'

Zechariah opened his mouth to answer the angel. But nothing came out. Not a word. Not a whisper. Not a sound!

So he staggered out of the temple—eyes wide open and lips shut tight. And it wasn't long before his wife came to him with the most amazing news.

'I'm going to have a baby!' she cried, tears of joy streaming down her face. 'After all these years, our prayers have been answered!'

Zechariah wanted to say, 'I know.' He wanted to say, 'The angel told me this would happen.' He wanted to shout 'Hooray!' But all he could do was smile. And that smile said more than enough!

A Surprise for Mary

That busy angel Gabriel went to work again.

Six months after Elizabeth discovered that she would have a child, he visited Elizabeth's cousin, Mary.

Mary and Elizabeth were quite different.

Elizabeth lived in the south, near the big city of Jerusalem. But Mary lived further north, in a little town called Nazareth.

Elizabeth was old. But Mary was young.

And Elizabeth had been married for many years, but Mary had never been married at all. She was engaged, however, to a carpenter named Joseph.

Mary was in her house, one day, dreaming of the wedding and the life that she and Joseph would share together. And that's when Gabriel appeared to her—bright and shiny, glowing and gold—just as he'd appeared to old Zechariah.

'Hello, Mary,' Gabriel said. 'God is with you and wants to do something very special for you.'

Mary didn't know what to think. She had never seen an angel before. And as for God wanting to do something special for her, well, she couldn't imagine what that might be. She was too scared to ask, and Gabriel could see the worry in her eyes.

'There's no need to be afraid,' he told her. 'God has chosen you for something wonderful. He wants you to be the mother of a little baby, a baby called Jesus.'

Mary looked more worried than ever. And puzzled too.

'I don't understand,' she said. 'How can I have a baby when I don't yet have a husband?'

Gabriel smiled. It was a warm smile. And a mysterious smile too.

'God's own Spirit will visit you,' he said. 'Like a welcome shadow on a warm summer's day, he will cover you and wrap himself around you. And the child who will spring to life in you will be God's child too.'

Mary was shaking now. Her eyes were wide open, amazed. Her mouth dropped open too. She had never heard anything like this before!

'I know this is hard to believe,' Gabriel went on. 'But God can do the most amazing things. Why, your own cousin, Elizabeth—that's right, Elizabeth, who could never have a child before—is expecting a baby too! Impossible? Not for God! So what do you say, Mary? Will you be the mother of God's Son?'

Mary shut her eyes. She shut her mouth too. She looked just as if she was praying.

What will Joseph think, she wondered,

when he hears about the child? He is bound to think the worst. And my parents too. Their plans, all their plans, will be ruined! And yet, God has a plan as well. And he has chosen me—me of all people—to be a part of that plan. What can I do but say yes?

And so Mary nodded. Eyes still shut, head bowed in prayer, she nodded.

'I will do it,' she said. 'I will be the mother of God's Son.'

And when she opened her eyes, the angel was gone.

Mary's Special Song

Mary had to tell someone!

The news that the angel Gabriel had given her was so amazing that it seemed almost too good to be true. So Mary hurried to visit the one person in the world she thought would understand—her cousin, Elizabeth.

Elizabeth was expecting a child of her own, remember? It was the son that Gabriel (that busy angel!) had promised to her and her husband, Zechariah.

Mary said 'Hello' to her cousin. But instead of saying 'Hello' back, Elizabeth said a surprised 'Ooh!'

'It's my baby!' she chuckled. 'When you said, 'Hello' he jumped! He jumped for joy, inside me! He knows—don't you see?—that the baby who is growing inside you is God's own Son.'

Elizabeth knew! She already knew! Even before Mary could tell her. Now Mary was more amazed than ever.

'God has done something wonderful for you,' said Elizabeth to Mary. 'And you have to trust that it will all come true—just as the angel told you.'

Mary nodded, 'I do. I really do.' And then she paused. And then she thought. And then she spoke again—as if she was making up a poem, or singing her own special song:

God has been so good to me
And I simply don't deserve it.
I'm nothing. A nobody.
Yet God has chosen me
To be the mother of his Son!
And one day—I'm sure of this—
Everyone will know my name
And be able to tell my story.
That's how God works, isn't it?
He knocks down the mighty and proud
And lifts up those who are small and weak.
He sends the rich away hungry.
And he feeds the hungry until they're full!
He has watched over his people, Israel,
From the time of our father, Abraham.
And now, praise God, he's watching over me!

When she had finished, Mary hugged her cousin, Elizabeth. Then she stayed with her for three months more, until Elizabeth's baby, John, was born, and then returned to her home in Nazareth.

A Name for the Baby

'What will you call him? Tell us his name!'

That's what everyone wanted to know: Elizabeth's sisters and brothers. Her nieces and nephews. Her cousins and neighbours and friends.

They had all come round to celebrate the birth of her son. They knew how long she had prayed. They knew how long she had waited. They had shared her surprised delight when she discovered that she would be having a child at last. And now they wanted to know his name.

'Perhaps you will name him after dear Uncle Ezra,' suggested one of her sisters.

'Or Grandfather Saul,' suggested another. 'Look! He has his smile!'

'Or what about our father?' added one of her brothers. 'It would be such an honour!'

And that's when Elizabeth held up her hand. 'We have already decided on a name,' she announced. 'We will call him John.'

The room went quiet for a moment. And then Elizabeth's oldest sister asked the question that everyone wanted to hear. 'But why do that? No one in our family has ever been called John.'

And that's when Elizabeth turned to her husband, Zechariah. He had been sitting there quietly (for that busy angel Gabriel had taken away his voice— remember?).

Zechariah nodded and smiled a mysterious smile. Then he picked up a writing tablet and wrote on it, clearly, so that everyone could see, 'His name is John.' And the minute he did so, Zechariah could speak again!

'Praise God!' he shouted. And he didn't stop talking until he had told them everything about the angel's visit and God's promise and how Gabriel had told him exactly what the child's name would be.

'This boy will be something special!' he concluded. 'God has great plans for him.'

And so God did. For when little John grew up, he went to live in the wilderness. He ate locusts for his supper and wild honey for his dessert. And he told God's people to change their ways and to be sorry for the wrong things that they had done, so that they would be ready to meet God's own special Son.

Joseph's Dream

Joseph the carpenter was not very happy. Not very happy at all.

The girl he had planned to marry was going to have a baby, but the baby was not his.

Mary had tried to explain. She had told him about the angel and what the angel had said. She had told him that the baby would be God's special Son. But Joseph did not believe her. And who could blame him? For the story was so amazing that Mary hardly believed it herself!

In the end, Joseph decided to call off the wedding—quietly, of course, so that Mary would not be embarrassed. And that was when that busy angel, Gabriel, decided to make another visit.

He appeared to Joseph in a dream—bright and shiny, glowing and gold—deep in the middle of the night.

'There's no need to be worried,' he said to Joseph. 'There's no need to be afraid. Everything Mary has told you is true. The baby she is carrying is God's own special Son. And when he is born, God wants you to call him Jesus. His name means "God saves". And when he grows up, that is exactly what he will do. He will be "God among us", "God come to save us" from everything that is wicked and wrong.'

When Joseph woke up, he knew exactly what to do. He went straight to Mary's house. He hugged her and told her he was sorry that he had not believed her. Then, just as soon as he could, he married her. And he took her home to be his wife.

Time to Be Counted

Mary counted the months.

One, two, three.

Four, five, six.

Seven, eight and nine.

It was almost time for her baby to be born!

Mary counted the blankets. Mary counted the towels. And then Mary smiled. For everything was ready—ready for the birth of God's own special Son.

But somebody else was counting too. And all Mary's plans were about to be ruined.

'It's the Emperor!' sighed Joseph, as he walked into the house. 'He wants to count everyone in the country. Everyone! And to make it easy for him, we have to go back to my home town.'

'*Your* home town?' cried Mary. 'But that means we have to go all the way to…'

'… Bethlehem!' sighed Joseph again. 'A week's journey, at least! And you with the baby coming.'

'I can't do it,' wept Mary. And the tears rolled down her cheeks.

One, two, three.

Four, five, six.

Seven, eight and nine.

Joseph counted each tear. Then he wiped them all away.

'But you must,' he said gently. 'It's the law.'

Then he held her and kissed her and he added more gently still, 'God is with you. Remember? That's what the angel told you. And if God is with you, then he will help you to make this journey. It's his promise,' said Joseph with a smile. 'So you can count on it!'

A Long Journey

One, two, three.

Four, five, six.

Seven, eight and nine.

Mary counted the miles. And the donkey's footsteps. And the number of times the little baby kicked inside her belly.

It was a long trip. And a hot trip. And she prayed that it would soon be over.

One, two, three.

Four, five, six.

Seven, eight and nine.

Mary knew, because she counted, that there were many more miles to go.

When they arrived, at last, in Bethlehem, Mary and Joseph looked for a place to stay.

One, two, three.

Four, five, six.

Seven, eight and nine.

They knocked on door after door. But at every door, the answer was the same. 'We have no room here! Go away!'

Mary began to cry.

'It's the baby!' she wept. 'The baby is coming. And I need somewhere to rest.'

So Joseph looked up and down the street once more.

One, two, three.

Four, five, six.

Seven, eight and nine.

And there, at house number ten, he found a door he had missed!

The door opened. The innkeeper smiled. But when Joseph asked if he had an empty room, the innkeeper sadly shook his head.

'Bethlehem is bursting,' he said with a sigh. 'We have no room at all.'

'But my wife…' Joseph pleaded. 'My wife is about to have a baby.'

'I can see that,' the innkeeper nodded. 'But I'm sorry, there's nothing I can do.' And he started to close the door.

'Please!' Joseph cried.

'Please!' wept Mary as well.

And that's when the door swung open again.

'There is a place,' nodded the innkeeper. 'Back behind the inn. It's nothing fancy, mind you. But it's warm and clean and dry. And you can have your baby safely there.'

So he led them to the stable. And there, among the animals, Mary finally lay down and gave birth to God's own special Son.

The Noisy Stable

It was nothing special. Just an ordinary stable. Filled with ordinary stable sounds.

The deep 'moo' of a big black cow.

The noisy 'hee-haw' of a little brown donkey.

The 'coo' of a dove, the 'baa' of a lamb, and the 'scrickety-scrack' of a spider, skittering along the wall.

But then there came another sound. An out-of-the-ordinary sound. A sound that had never been heard in this stable before—the sharp 'waa-waa!' of a newborn baby.

It was Mary's baby, of course. The baby the angel Gabriel had promised her. But there was nothing ordinary about him. For he was Jesus, God's own special Son.

The cow went 'moo'.

The donkey brayed 'hee-haw'.

The dove called 'coo', the lamb cried 'baa', and the spider skittered, 'scrickety-scrack', back into his web.

It was just an ordinary stable. With ordinary stable sounds…

And one extraordinary baby boy!

A Flock of Angels

That busy angel, Gabriel, had one more Christmas job to do. He had to tell somebody that the baby, Jesus, had been born.

He could have told a powerful somebody—like the king.

He could have told a religious somebody—like the high priest.

Or he could have told a wealthy somebody—like the richest man in Bethlehem.

But instead he told the shepherds—plain and ordinary somebodies. Somebodies like you and me!

They were watching their sheep, out on a hillside. It was late. It was dark. And some of them just wanted to drop off to sleep.

And that's when Gabriel appeared—bright and shiny, glowing and gold—just as he had appeared to Mary and to Zechariah.

'Don't be afraid!' he said to the shepherds, and he smiled when he realized how silly that sounded.

Of course they were afraid! Who wouldn't be? They had never seen an angel before. And so they were trembling and shaking, just like frightened sheep.

'I have good news for you!' Gabriel explained. 'God has sent someone very special, to bring joy to this dark world. And tonight that someone has been born—not far from here, in Bethlehem! Go, and you will find him, a baby bundled up tight and lying in a manger.'

And then, suddenly, Gabriel was not alone. The angels that joined him looked like sheep, at first, bright against the dark sky—reflections of the beasts on the hill below. But as the shepherds watched, the angels spread their wings and began to sing:

'Glory to God in heaven,
And peace to men on earth!'

And when they had finished, they disappeared, leaving the shepherds alone.

It took no time at all. The shepherds leaped to their feet and went to Bethlehem. There they found Mary and Joseph, and the baby in the manger. And when they described what they had seen—to the innkeeper and his wife and anyone else who would listen—everyone wondered and was amazed. Everyone but Mary, that is, who nodded and smiled as if she had expected just this sort of thing to happen.

Then, singing and laughing, the shepherds went back to the hills. But they kept their eyes trained on the sky, just in case another bright flock of angels should appear!

The Star That Went Zoom!

Twinkle-twinkle, went the stars. And the star-watchers nodded and smiled.

'There's a pretty one!' the first star-watcher said.

'And look how brightly that one is shining,' said the second star-watcher.

'And the big one—the big one over there,' cried the third star-watcher. 'I don't think I've ever seen one so huge!'

Twinkle-twinkle, went the stars. And then one of the stars went Zoom!

'Did you see that?' asked the first star-watcher.

'Couldn't miss it!' said the second.

'What do you suppose it means?' wondered the third. So they all ran for their special star-watching books.

Twinkle-twinkle, went the stars. And the star-watchers read and searched and scratched their heads. 'It's not an earthquake,' said the first star-watcher. 'We can be grateful for that!'

'And it's not a flood, either,' said the second.

And that's when the third star-watcher went 'Aha! I've found it! A zooming star means that, somewhere, a new king has been born!'

'But where?' asked the other star-watchers.

'There's no way to tell,' said the third star-watcher, 'unless we follow the star and see where it stops.'

'Then let's do it!' said the first star-watcher, putting on his hat.

'Sounds good to me,' said the second, as he pulled on his long coat.

'I'll need to find someone to mind the cat,' said the third. 'But I'd like to go as well.'

And so the star-watchers gathered their servants and loaded their camels. And with the stars twinkle-twinkling above, they set off after that special star—the star that went Zoom!

The Star-watchers' Journey

The star zoomed left. The star zoomed right. Over hills it zoomed, and deserts and rivers and mountain peaks.

The star-watchers did their best to zoom after it. But the hills were high, and the deserts were hot. The rivers were deep, and the mountain peaks were hard to climb. And that was why it took them so long to follow the star.

For days and weeks and months they travelled, until finally, the star stopped, and they found themselves in Judea, at the edge of the Great Sea.

'This is the land of the Jews,' said the first star-watcher.

'Then the baby must be their new king,' said the second.

'So let's find the palace,' suggested the third star-watcher, 'and give him the honour he deserves.'

They thought they had it all worked out, and so the star-watchers headed for Jerusalem and the palace of the king. But what they failed to notice was that the star had zoomed somewhere else!

The star-watchers asked everyone they met.

'We have come from the East,' they explained. 'We are looking for a king. Perhaps you could help us find him—the newborn King of the Jews.'

Everyone was surprised by the question. And no one more than King Herod.

'What do they mean?' he shouted at his advisers. 'I am the King of the Jews!'

'Y-Yes, of c-course,' stammered the frightened men. 'B-But perhaps they are looking for the special king—the one God promised us, many years ago.'

'And where would they find such a king?' Herod growled.

'In B-Bethlehem,' the advisers stammered again. 'At least, that's what the prophets say.'

'I see,' Herod muttered. And then his eyes began to twinkle—twinkle like two dark stars. 'Send for these star-watchers,' he commanded. 'I have something to ask them.'

The star-watchers came as quickly as they could. And once Herod had sent away his advisers, he leaned over to the star-watchers and whispered, 'The king you are looking for is in the town of Bethlehem. I want you to go there—it's not far—and when you have found him, I want you to return and tell me exactly where he is—so that I might honour him too.'

The star-watchers nodded and bowed. They thanked the king and then headed straight for Bethlehem. But what they did not know was that Herod was an evil king—a king determined to kill anyone who tried to take his throne—even a little baby boy in Bethlehem!

Gifts for a King

When the star-watchers arrived in Bethlehem, the star was already waiting for them there. But it was no longer zooming. Instead, it crept along slowly, leading them through the narrow streets of the town. And then, suddenly, it stopped, and hovered silently over a very ordinary-looking house.

'This must be the place,' said the first star-watcher.

'It doesn't look much like a palace,' said the second.

'Well, we shall have to go in and see for ourselves,' said the third. And he knocked, politely, on the door.

An ordinary-looking man opened the door—a man as ordinary as the house.

'We're very sorry,' said the first star-watcher. 'We must have the wrong place.'

'Forgive us for troubling you,' apologized the second.

'But the star…' whispered the third star-watcher to the others, 'The star is right overhead.' And then he turned to the man at the door. 'We're looking for a king—the newborn King of the Jews. I don't suppose you have a baby here?'

And with that, the ordinary-looking man smiled. A secret smile. A knowing smile.

For this man was Joseph.

'As a matter of fact, we do,' he said. 'Little Jesus is almost a year old, now, but I think he's the one you're looking for.'

The star-watchers filed into the house. The child was sitting on his mother's lap, playing with her fingers. And as soon as they saw him, they knew they were in the right place.

One by one, the star-watchers fell to their knees before him. Then they gave him presents—presents they had brought all the way from the East. But they weren't the kind of presents that most people give to babies. No rattles or building blocks or soft toys.

No, they were presents fit for a king:

Bright, shiny gold.

A rich perfume called myrrh.

And frankincense, a sweet-smelling oil.

The baby patted the gold, and the jar that held the oil. But when he very nearly tipped over the bottle of perfume, his mother gently took his hand. 'Thank you,' she said to the star-watchers. 'It was kind of you to come.'

And so the star-watchers stood and bowed and said their goodbyes. It was too late to return to Jerusalem, so they set up their tents on the outskirts of town. But as they lay there asleep, each of the star-watchers had a dream. There was a visitor, bright and shiny, glowing and gold (that busy angel, Gabriel, perhaps?). And the visitor had a message.

'King Herod wants to kill the child,' the message warned them. 'You must not return to him. Go back to your homes, instead. Go quickly! And you will save the child's life.'

So the star-watchers rose at once. They folded their tents. They loaded their camels. And, rubbing the sleep from their eyes, they started for home, the stars twinkle-twinkling like gold to light their way.

King Herod's Evil Plan

King Herod frowned.

King Herod scowled.

King Herod clenched his teeth and scrunched up his face.

And then King Herod shouted. 'THE STAR-WATCHERS ARE GONE!?'

'Y-yes, Your Majesty,' his advisers muttered. 'At least that is what we have heard.'

'But they were supposed to return to me! They were supposed to tell me where I could find this newborn king!'

'W-well, we know he's in Bethlehem,' said the advisers.

'Of course he's in Bethlehem!' the king shouted again. 'Along with hundreds of other babies…' And as soon as he'd said it, the king's face changed.

He no longer frowned.

He no longer scowled.

He no longer clenched his teeth or scrunched up his face.

No, King Herod began to smile—a dark and cruel smile.

'Leave me!' he commanded. 'And send in the captain of my guard.'

That smile was still on Herod's face when the captain entered and bowed.

'I have a job for you,' the king explained. 'I want you to go to Bethlehem and kill… oh, let us say, every male child two years old and under.'

The captain did not smile.

He did not frown, either.

He just stood there with his lips pressed tightly together. His eyes showed his surprise, however, for this was the most awful thing he had ever heard.

'Well, get on with it!'

the king commanded. 'You have your orders. And there are plenty of others,' he added, 'who would love to have your job.'

And so the captain left and rounded up his soldiers. And they set off to kill all of Bethlehem's baby boys.

Joseph slept. He had a sweet, sleepy smile on his face. But his smile turned to a worried frown when the visitor appeared to him in a dream. It was that busy angel, Gabriel, again. 'Get up, Joseph,' he said. 'Take the child and his mother and go to Egypt. Herod's soldiers are on the way. And they mean to kill the boy.'

Joseph got up at once. He nudged Mary awake and quietly they packed their things. Then she bundled up the sleeping Jesus and, together, they slipped off into the night.

They stayed in Egypt until King Herod died. Then they returned to Nazareth where Jesus grew up— the son of a carpenter and God's own special Son as well!

Stories about Christmas Traditions

All around the world people celebrate Christmas in different ways, often continuing traditions that began centuries ago. Here is a selection of stories—some old and some new—showing how some popular Christmas customs began.

Old Befana

Shoop, shoop, shoop. Old Befana swept the floor.

Shoop, shoop, shoop. She swept out the cupboards too.

Shoop, shoop, shoop. Old Befana swept up every bit of dirt, every tumbling dustball, and every little crumb.

Old Befana's house was spotless! And her front step too. And the path that led to the road.

Sweeping was all that Old Befana did. It was all that Old Befana loved. And so she was annoyed when, early one morning, in the midst of her sweeping, she was interrupted by a loud Bang, bang, bang! on the door.

She opened the door, the broom still in her hand. And she was greeted by three tall, tired strangers.

'We have travelled all night,' said the first stranger.

'We are following a star,' explained the second.

'And we need somewhere to sleep,' begged the third.

Old Befana looked at the three men. They were very well dressed. There were jewels on their hats and on their gowns and on the chains that hung round their necks. They could

have been rich merchants, or wizards, or kings. In any case, they did not look like robbers. And as for her sweeping—well, the bedroom had already been swept for the day. So she nodded her head and welcomed them in.

She showed them the way to the bedroom, and when she looked in on them a few minutes later, she discovered that they were all fast asleep in one bed—the covers pulled up tight under their big beards!

Old Befana returned to her sweeping.

Shoop, shoop, shoop. She swept the kitchen.

Shoop, shoop, shoop. She swept the living room too.

Shoop, shoop, shoop. She swept the step and the path to the road.

And all the while she swept, she wondered.

'Where do they come from? Where are they going? And why do they sleep all day?'

So when, at last, the three strangers awoke, she asked them.

'We come from the East,' said the first stranger, 'and travel all night.'

'We are following a star,' said the second.

'A star that will lead us to the King of all Kings,' explained the third. 'A king who is but a little child!'

Then the three strangers made Old Befana a most unusual offer.

'Since you have been so kind to us…' began the first stranger.

'And since you have given us a place to rest…' continued the second.

'We would like you to come with us!' invited the third, 'to see this king and to bring him gifts!'

Old Befana was so surprised that she nearly dropped her broom.

39

What an adventure! she thought. To follow a star and find a king!

But then she looked at her broom. And she looked around her house. And it didn't take her long to imagine how dusty everything would be, if she ceased her sweeping for even one day.

So she sadly shook her head and said, 'No, thank you.' And the three strangers walked off into the night.

Old Befana went to sleep, but her dreams were interrupted by visions of strangers and stars and kings. The next morning, she picked up her broom, as usual, but try as she might, she could not keep her mind on her sweeping.

Shoop, shoop, shoop. She swept the living room. But all she could think of was the strangers' invitation.

Shoop, shoop. She swept the kitchen. But all she could think of was that wandering star.

Shoop. She swept the front step. But all she could think of was the little king—who was down that road, somewhere, in a house, with a path and a step like hers.

And that's when she decided she would join the strangers after all. So with the broom in one hand, and an apron full of little gifts, she set off down the road.

She walked and she walked. She searched and she searched. But, sadly, Old Befana never did find the three strangers. And, so they say, she is walking still—with a broom in her hand and with an apron full of gifts. And each Christmas, she walks up every path, climbs up every step and visits every house. And wherever she finds a child, she leaves a little gift. For she never can be certain which of those children is the 'King of all Kings'!

Brother Froilan's Carvings

Brother Froilan carved a piglet. Brother Froilan carved a duck. Brother Froilan carved a chicken and a dog and a cat, and when he had finished each one, the children cried out, 'Give it to me, Brother Froilan! Give it to me!'

Brother Froilan made the children happy. But Brother Froilan was not very happy himself. He had left his home and come to Spain, many months before, to tell the people there about God. But no one seemed very interested. As far as he could tell, they were too afraid of their gods of wind and earth and fire to take much notice of the God Brother Froilan had come to share with them—the God of Love.

And so he carved his little animals, and hoped, at least, to win the children's trust—until, one spring morning, suddenly Brother Froilan had an idea.

There are animals in the Christmas story, he thought. They were there when God's Son, Jesus, was born.

So, that very morning, Brother Froilan began to carve a little donkey.

'Who is the donkey for?' asked one of the children.

'It's for Mary,' answered Brother Froilan.

'But there is no one named Mary here,' said another child, looking around.

'Ah,' Brother Froilan smiled mysteriously, 'but there was a Mary once, many years ago, who needed to get to Bethlehem.'

'Bethlehem?' asked another child. And so the story began.

The next day, Brother Froilan carved a cow, and told the children about the baby born in a stable.

42

A flock of wooden sheep soon followed. And a carved angel too. And the children sat, eyes open with wonder, as the monk described the heavenly visitors who came to tell their good news to the shepherds.

As spring blossomed into summer, a camel appeared. And then another. And another still. And Brother Froilan explained how the camels' riders had journeyed many miles, following a star, just to catch a glimpse of this special child—a child sent by the God of Love himself to bring his goodness and his peace into the world.

When the story was finished, the children shouted, as children often do, 'Again! Again! Tell it again!'

And so Brother Froilan picked up another piece of wood and started on another donkey.

And by the time summer ripened into a crisp and crunchy autumn, he had told the story so many times

that the floor of his little hut was covered with donkeys and camels and cows. And Marys and Josephs and wise men too.

Yes, the children had often asked for the little figures. But Brother Froilan had always carved them something else instead, and said, very mysteriously, 'I'm saving these. Saving them for the time when the world grows cold and dark.'

That time finally arrived—Christmas time! And at every place where the footpaths crossed, Brother Froilan built a little stable and perched it on a stump or in the crook of some small tree. He filled each one with his little carvings, and when the people walked by, they would wonder and ask, 'What is that?'

And that is when their children would smile mysteriously and say, 'That's Mary, who had to go to Bethlehem. That is the donkey she rode on. Those are the shepherds who saw an angel, and the wise men who followed a star. And there, in the crib in the middle, is the Son of the God of Love.'

And that is how a single monk—with a little knife and some wood and a love for children —brought the story of Jesus to Spain.

Kind Bishop Nicholas

Nicholas had never heard such a sad story. He had been the bishop of Myra for many years, teaching and leading and caring for the Christians in that city. He had helped many people through many difficult times. But when he heard the story of the three young girls—well, it almost broke his heart.

'Their father has no money,' a neighbour had explained. 'The only way he can take care of the rest of the family is to sell three of his daughters into slavery.'

'Slavery?' sighed Nicholas. 'No! We cannot let that happen!'

'But what can we do?' asked the neighbour.

'I don't have the money, nor does anyone I know. Besides, the father would be humiliated if anyone else found out. He made me promise not to tell, and I have only broken that promise for the sake of those girls.'

'I understand,' Nicholas nodded. 'Leave it with me. I'll see what I can do.'

Bishop Nicholas took the long way home that night. He walked slowly down the narrow streets. People greeted him, as they always did, 'Hello, Bishop Nicholas!' 'How are you, Bishop Nicholas?' But instead of his usual jolly smile, all they received was a polite nod. The Bishop was deep in thought.

When he arrived home, the time for thinking was over. Now it was time to act. And Bishop Nicholas knew exactly what he had to do. He opened a box—a special money box he had hidden beneath the floor—and he took out every coin inside it.

It was all that remained of his family's fortune—a fortune that Nicholas had given away, coin by coin and year by year, to the needy people of Myra. There was enough left, just enough he hoped, to keep the girls from being sold as slaves. But that was only half the problem. How would he get the money to their father without the man knowing that Nicholas had discovered his secret?

Bishop Nicholas looked hard at the pile of money. Then he started to move it around.

Three girls. Three piles.

Three piles. Three… bags.

Of course! Nicholas had his idea now.

He put each pile into a little leather bag, then tied each bag shut at the top. Then he waited until it was dark—so dark that there would be no one left on the streets. And with the three little bags tucked inside his robes, he wandered back through the town.

Nicholas chuckled to himself, as he walked along. This was a great plan! Soon he came to the house. There were no lamps lit. Everyone was asleep. And so Bishop Nicholas put his plan into action. He pulled the little bags from

under his robe, then he tossed them—one, two, three—through an open window. Then, with another chuckle, he hurried back to his home.

When the family woke up the next morning, they found the three bags on the floor. Where had they come from? Who had put them there? And what was in them? No one could answer the first two questions, but when the girls insisted on opening the bags, they all discovered the answer to the third.

'Praise God!' the father shouted. 'Our prayers have been answered! And our family can stay together!'

No one knows how the truth got out. Perhaps it was the neighbour who told.

Or maybe someone else was out there in the dark—someone who saw the Bishop tossing his little gifts through the window.

What we do know is that Nicholas grew famous for the care he showed to children. The stories about him spread across the world and, many years after his death, he was made a saint. Then, somehow, his name was linked with another mysterious midnight traveller—a jolly, kind man who leaves gifts for children and then disappears into the dark!

The Littlest Camel

'Hurry along!' snorted the Big Brown Camel —from the back of the caravan. 'Hurry along, or we'll never catch up!'

'He's going as fast as he can!' said Mother Camel. 'You can't ask for more than that.'

And the Littlest Camel? The Littlest Camel said nothing. For it was all he could do to keep his little legs moving.

Up the sand dunes and down the sand dunes.

Over the mountains and across the rocky plains.

He had done nothing but walk for weeks. And when the walking was over, he would sleep—fast and deep—snuggled at his mother's side.

'He shouldn't even be here!' grunted the Big Brown Camel. And he spat on the dusty track. 'He's not big enough to carry anything. And he's slow. Much too slow!'

'But it's not his fault!' said Mother Camel. 'How many times do I have to tell you? The camel driver made a mistake. He picked me out, at the market—the same place where he bought you—but he didn't see my baby beside me. And by the time we reached the desert and he noticed, it was too late to turn back.'

'Well, I'm not going to get left behind. I promise you that!' the Big Brown Camel grunted.

Again, the Littlest Camel didn't say a word. He just tried to keep his legs moving. One, two, three, four. One, two, three, four.

And that's when somebody shouted, 'The star has stopped! Look, there's the town.'

'It won't be long now, dear,' said Mother Camel. And the Littlest Camel smiled. He couldn't wait to rest his weary legs. But as they entered the town, everyone started to speed

up, for the men at the front of the caravan were anxious to reach their destination.

Maybe that's why it happened. Or perhaps it was because the Big Brown Camel was in such a hurry. But when they turned a corner in one of Bethlehem's narrow streets, the Littlest Camel tripped and fell tumbling to the ground.

The Big Brown Camel stepped right over him. 'I'm not waiting for you!' he grunted.

And even though Mother Camel turned and tried to stop, the camel driver was in such a rush that he whipped her back into the line.

The Littlest Camel picked himself up, leg by bony leg. Then he ran as fast as those legs would carry him, after his mother and the rest of the caravan. Through the streets he followed them, always just that bit too far behind.

But when they finally stopped—beasts and men alike, falling on their knees before a simple stable—the Littlest Camel could not slow down! And so he tripped and tumbled

one more time—past camels and servants and three men with bright gifts—and landed head-first at the foot of a wooden manger.

The Littlest Camel shook his head.

The Littlest Camel opened his eyes.

The Littlest Camel was face-to-face with a little baby!

The baby smiled at him and patted his camel nose.

And that's when the camel heard these words: 'Well done, little camel. You travelled far to see my Son. And you never gave up. So from now on, it will be a camel, the Littlest Camel, who will bring gifts to the children of this land.'

And that is why, to this day, children in the Middle East receive their Christmas gifts from the back of a camel—a little camel, just like the one who brought joy to the child in the manger.

Wenceslas' Winter Walk

It was the day after Christmas—St Stephen's Day—and Wenceslas, the King of Bohemia, was looking out through his palace window. A fire blazed behind him. His big belly was full. And his heart was bursting with the joy of the season!

And then King Wenceslas saw something out in the snowy fields. It might have been a wild animal, or somebody's stray dog. But as he looked closer, straining his eyes through the falling snow, he realized that it was a man!

Wenceslas called for one of his young servants—a page.

'Who is that?' he asked. And he pointed out the window.

The page peered through the falling snow as well.

'It's just an old peasant,' he shrugged. 'Vladimir, I think. Probably looking for firewood.'

The king studied the man, and the blustery winter weather too. Then he thought of all

the riches stored up inside his palace walls.

'Where does he live?' the king asked.

'Far from here—at the foot of the mountain,' the page answered. 'Why do you ask?'

'Because we are going to help him,' said the king, slapping the little page on the back. 'Bring me food! Bring me wine! Bring me pine logs!' the king commanded. 'We are going to follow him home!'

'But, your guests…' the page protested. 'Your Christmas celebrations…'

'How can I celebrate,' the king sighed, 'when that poor man cannot even keep warm? Food! Wine! Logs!' he commanded again. And he said it so firmly this time that the page dared say no more.

Off through the snow they trudged—king and page, side by side, their arms filled with gifts. The wind howled. The snow came tumbling down. The peasant's house was a long way off. And soon the page grew tired and started to lag behind.

'Your Majesty!' he shouted through the wind. 'I don't think I can go any further. I'm very tired and my feet are so cold I can hardly feel them!'

King Wenceslas stopped to think. He wanted to help the poor peasant. But it wasn't worth risking the life of his young page. He was about to send him back home, in fact, when the king had an idea.

'Walk behind me, boy,' he said kindly. 'Put your feet in my footprints. And let's see if that is any help.'

So that is what they did. And when the page put his feet in his master's footprints, it seemed to him as if the ground underneath was warm—warmed by the steps of the king!

It was easy to walk in the snow now. And they were soon at the peasant's house. Old Vladimir couldn't believe it when the king appeared at his door. And he was even more shocked when the king laid the gifts before him and bellowed, 'Food! Wine! Logs! And a Merry Christmas!'

The story of King Wenceslas and his winter walk soon spread round and about (was it the page who first told it?), and many years later it was turned into a song—a song that many people sing at Christmas still.

Good King Wenceslas looked out,
On the feast of Stephen,
When the snow lay round about,
Deep and crisp and even:
Brightly shone the moon that night,
Though the frost was cruel,
When a poor man came in sight,
Gathering winter fuel.

'Hither, page, and stand by me,
If thou know'st it, telling,
Yonder peasant, who is he?
Where and what his dwelling?'
'Sire, he lives a good league hence,
Underneath the mountain,
Right against the forest fence,
By St Agnes' fountain.'

'Bring me flesh, and bring me wine,
Bring me pine logs hither:
Thou and I will see him dine,
When we bear them thither.'
Page and monarch, forth they went,
Forth they went together;
Through the rude wind's wild lament
And the bitter weather.

'Sire, the night is darker now,
And the wind blows stronger;
Fails my heart, I know not how;
I can go no longer.'
'Mark my footsteps, good my page;
Tread thou in them boldly:
Thou shalt find the winter's rage
Freeze thy blood less coldly.'

In his master's steps he trod,
Where the snow lay dinted;
Heat was in the very sod
Which the Saint had printed.
Therefore, Christian men, be sure,
Wealth or rank possessing,
Ye who now will bless the poor,
Shall yourselves find blessing.

Johnny's Socks

Long ago, in the hills of Tennessee, there lived three boys—Ronny and Donny and Johnny. They were brothers, who lived with their mama in a little rundown cabin.

Ronny was the oldest—and the smartest too. Donny was the strongest. And as for Johnny, well, he had a friendly smile and a good heart, but there was no escaping the fact that he wasn't very bright. And because of that, his older brothers never stopped playing tricks on him.

One Christmas Eve, as the brothers sat in front of the fireplace, Ronny turned to Johnny and said, 'Santa Claus is coming tonight!'

'Yep,' said Johnny with a smile.

'And he's bringing us presents,' Ronny continued.

'Yep,' Johnny smiled again.

And then Ronny glanced at Donny and grinned a mischievous grin. 'He'll be coming down that chimney, Johnny,' he said. 'And if somebody don't do something, old Santa Claus is gonna land on top of that fire!'

Johnny's smile dropped right off his face. 'Oh no!' he hollered. And, because he had a good heart, Johnny grabbed a bucket of water and threw it right on that fire.

The fire sizzled to nothing and belched out a cloud of black smoke that filled the room. Johnny's brothers laughed and rolled all over the floor. But then Johnny's mother walked through the door.

'Johnny!' she hollered. 'What have you been up to?'

Johnny stood there—covered in soot and smelling of smoke. 'Fireplace… save… Santa Claus,' he tried to explain. But his brothers interrupted him.

'He put out the fire!' said Ronny.

'He's not very bright, you know,' added Donny.

And so their mother picked up her big broom and chased Johnny upstairs into his room.

'Get out of those filthy clothes!' she hollered. 'I don't want to see you again until morning!' And she went and lit the fire again.

So Johnny took off his dirty clothes and he climbed into his bed. And not a minute later, there came a knock at his door. It was Donny.

'Johnny,' Donny whispered through the keyhole. 'Santa Claus is coming tonight.'

'Yep,' Johnny sighed.

'And he's gonna bring us presents,' Donny continued.

'Yep,' said Johnny, a little happier now.

And then Donny grinned at Ronny, who was sitting there quietly beside him.

'But Santa Claus won't be able to find us,' said Donny, 'unless there's somebody outside to wave at him.'

'Oh no!' Johnny hollered, his good heart beating away again. And forgetting all that his mother had said, he rushed out of his room, down the stairs and out the front door!

Johnny's mother was in the kitchen, putting the finishing touches on her famous Christmas fruitcake. So she hadn't seen a thing. Well, not until Ronny tapped her on the shoulder and said, 'Johnny's at it again, Ma. Look what he's doing.' And he led her to the front window.

Johnny was waving—waving to the sky—with nothing on but his long johns and an old pair of socks.

'He's not very bright, you know,' added Donny. But the angry woman had already thrown open the front door.

'Johnny!' she shouted, shaking her big broom. 'Johnny, get in here this minute!'

She wrapped him up in a warm blanket. She pulled off his soaking-wet socks. She sat him down before the fire. Then she scolded him some more.

'When you get yourself dry,' she hollered, 'you will go to your room and stay there— tonight and tomorrow too!'

'But tomorrow's Christmas!' wept Johnny.

'Christmas is for good boys!' his mother said. 'Boys who do what their mama tells them! Boys like your brothers!' Then she stomped back into the kitchen.

Johnny had never been so unhappy. But that didn't keep his brothers from trying to make him unhappier still!

'Johnny,' said Ronny. 'Your socks are soaking wet.'

'Johnny,' said Donny. 'We'd better dry them off.' And he dangled them above the fire.

'No!' hollered Johnny. 'If my socks get all burned up, Mama will *never* let me out of my room!'

'We wouldn't want that to happen,' said Ronny, and he held up a hammer.

'Not for a minute,' added Donny, and he pulled some nails from his pocket.

'Oh, I see!' Johnny smiled. 'If I nail my socks over the fire, they won't get all burned up! You boys are so clever!' And with that, he picked up the hammer and nailed his socks to the mantelpiece.

Johnny's mother heard the hammering, of course. And it wasn't long before that big broom was chasing him back into his room again.

'And don't come out till New Year's Eve!' his mama hollered, while Ronny and Donny howled with laughter.

The next morning, as Johnny waited sadly in his room, the rest of the family marched downstairs to see what Santa Claus had left. Under the scrawny tree, where the presents usually were, there was nothing. But the socks nailed up to the mantelpiece were stretched almost to bursting!

'Me first!' hollered Ronny.

'No, me first!' Donny hollered back.

'Wait just a minute!' hollered their mama, waving her big broom. 'There's a note pinned to them socks. And it appears to be addressed to me.'

'Dear Mama,' the note read, 'those two boys of yours, Ronny and Donny, were responsible for all your troubles last night. They tricked poor Johnny (he's not that bright, you know!). But he has a good heart, and that's why all the presents in these stretched-out old socks are for him! Thanks for the fruitcake, by the way. Your friend, Santa Claus.'

Well, as soon as Mama put down the note, that big broom of hers started flying. She chased those boys up one mountainside and down another.

And so, every Christmas after that, Johnny nailed his old socks above the fire. His brothers did too. So did his mama. And, as silly as it might seem, some folks are doing it still!

A Flower for Christmas

Everyone was walking to the church. Every-one in the little Mexican town. Their arms were heavy with gifts—fruit and vegetables and sweets—for it was Christmas Eve and everyone was expected to bring a present for the Christ Child.

Manuel watched them all walk by. He watched them laugh. He watched them sing. He watched the way they shared their excitement and joy.

But all he could do was to wipe the tears from his dirty face, for Manuel was a child of the streets—a poor orphan boy with nothing at all to bring.

He had tried begging for something, but the people had only laughed. 'You say you want it for the Christ Child?' they sneered. 'We know your kind. You'll just keep it for yourself!'

He had thought about stealing something too. But stealing? For the Christ Child? Surely that would be worse than bringing no gift at all.

And so he kept his distance. And when the crowd had shuffled into the church, and when the doors had been shut behind them, he crept to an open window and peered in.

Everything was so beautiful—the candles, the decorations and the gifts! There were hundreds of them, piled up round the statue of the Christ Child and his mother.

But the longer Manuel looked, the sadder he felt, until finally, he fell to his knees and he prayed, 'Dear Christ Child, I am not like the people in the church. I have nothing to bring to you this Christmas Eve. So please accept my prayer. And my tears as well. For they are all I have to give you.'

Manuel wiped his face dry again. Then he

opened his eyes. And there, where his tears had fallen, was a flower. A flower that had not been there before. Gold as the star that shone over Bethlehem, that's how bright the flower was. And surrounding it, there were leaves as red as blood!

'It's a miracle!' Manuel cried. And he scooped up the flower, roots and all, and ran into the church.

'Look!' he shouted, running down the aisle. 'Look! I have a gift for the Christ Child too!'

Some people whispered and moaned. They did not like their service interrupted. But when they saw the flower, their groans turned to sighs of wonder.

'It is a miracle, indeed!' the priest agreed. 'A flower such as I have never seen!'

And so it was that Manuel's poinsettia became known by the special name of 'The Flower of the Holy Night'!

The First Christmas Tree

Boniface was walking through the woods. It was winter. It was cold. But even though Boniface was desperate for a hot drink and a warm fire, he kept on walking. For it was his job to travel, from one end of England to the other, telling the people about Jesus. Boniface heard a cry. It was a child's cry. A frightened cry. So Boniface stopped walking and began to run.

The branches snapped at his face. The wind howled about him. But he was getting closer, he could tell, for the child's cries were growing louder.

At last, Boniface stumbled into a clearing. There, gathered at the foot of an oak tree, was a group of men—and the child's cry came from the midst of them.

'Stop!' Boniface shouted. 'Stop what you are doing! Now!'

The men turned towards him. Their faces were painted with strange and frightening patterns and each one held a weapon.

'Go away!' one of them called back. 'This is no business of yours!'

'Yes it is!' Boniface replied. 'For I can tell, by your dress and by your face-paint, that you are Druids. And if I am not mistaken, you intend to kill that boy and offer him as a sacrifice to one of your tree gods.'

'The god of the oak demands it!' one Druid argued. 'And we are here to serve him.'

'Well, I serve another God!' argued Boniface. 'A God who does not approve of the killing of children.' And with that, he grabbed an axe and began to chop at the base of the oak tree. One of the Druids went to stop him, but the leader held him back.

'Wait,' he said with a sneer. 'The god of the oak tree will punish him soon enough!'

Boniface chopped and chopped. He chopped until he had chopped that oak tree down. And as it crashed to the forest floor, the Druids began to tremble.

'I don't understand,' said their leader. 'The god in the oak tree did nothing to protect himself—and nothing to punish you!'

'That's because there is no god *in* the tree!' Boniface explained. 'There is only one God—the God who *made* the tree, and everything else in this world. The God who does not demand the sacrifice of our sons. No, for he has already sacrificed his own Son, Jesus—sacrificed him on a tree—to take away all that is wrong in this world.'

'He sacrificed his own son?' said the Druid leader in wonder.

'Yes,' nodded Boniface. 'And more amazing than that, he brought his Son back to life again, so that we could live for ever too!'

And then Boniface pointed to a tree. Not the fallen oak, but a bright furry evergreen. 'If you want to remember the God I serve,' Boniface said, 'you could use that tree—the tree that never dies. Decorate it, and use it to celebrate the birth of Jesus—the Son of God, who lives for ever!'

So that's what the Druids did. And some people say that was the very first Christmas tree!

The Icicles

Through the woods they walked—Joseph and Mary and little Jesus.

King Herod was dead. They were safe at last. And so they were going home—all the way from Egypt to Nazareth.

The days were warm enough. Too warm, sometimes. So they would rest, when they could, in some welcoming shadow.

But the nights were cold—especially the nights in the hills. And this night was the coldest of them all!

The trees looked down on them and shook their leafless branches.

'They'll freeze to death!' said the cedar.

'They must find shelter,' said the birch.

'And look at the little boy,' sighed the pine tree. 'He can hardly keep from shivering.'

'But what can we do?' asked the cedar. 'My branches are bare. The wind will blow right through them.'

'Mine are no better,' nodded the birch.

And then they both looked at the pine tree.

'Of course!' she shouted. 'Why didn't I think of it myself?' And at once, she began to shake her furry boughs—so hard and so strong that Mary and Joseph could not fail to notice her.

'Look!' cried Joseph. 'A pine tree! If we huddle together beneath the branches, perhaps we can keep the wind out, and stay warm through the night.'

Mary agreed. And little Jesus just shivered. So the three of them crept under the prickly pine boughs and wrapped themselves up in their blankets.

The wind blew and blew.

The night grew frosty and sharp. Snowflakes began to fall. But through it all, Joseph and Mary and little Jesus slept safe and warm.

'They're still alive!' said the cedar to the pine tree.

'I think you've saved them!' added the birch.

And then the pine tree heard another voice—the glad song of a passing angel.

'Well done, pine tree!' the angel sang. 'For your warm boughs have sheltered the Son of God, himself!'

The pine tree could hardly believe it. And in her excitement, she began to weep— tears of happiness, tears of joy! The tears trickled down her bushy branches. And as they trickled, they froze— froze in long, icy strands, all the way down to the ground.

When Mary and Joseph and Jesus awoke the next morning, they crawled out from under the tree. And what they saw made the little boy jump with delight.

'Look!' he called. 'Look at all the pretty icicles.'

And so they were, shining like diamonds in the morning sun.

And perhaps that is why some people still dress their Christmas trees with icicle decorations—in memory of that clever pine tree and her beautiful frozen tears.

The First Tinsel

It was Christmas Eve and, at last, everything was quiet.

The children had finally forced themselves to sleep.

Mother and Father were snoring away, exhausted, in their bed.

And even the mice were snuggled safe in their holes.

So that's when the spiders came out—crawling through the crack in the corner of the ceiling.

'The coast is clear!' called Mr Spider.

'I'm coming as fast as I can!' called his wife in return.

It was the same every night. They would anchor two long, sticky strands to the ceiling, and swing across the room, down to the floor on the other side. Then they would snip the silky strands and explore! Up and down the curtains they would go, over and under each chair. And if, along the way, they happened to stumble across a wandering fly or a wayward ant, then they would enjoy a midnight snack as well!

'Hang on tight!' said Mr Spider.

'Eight legs' worth!' said Mrs Spider in return.

And with a leap and a 'Yahoo!' the spiders sailed across the room.

They should have reached the far end of the room, just as normal. But it was Christmas Eve, remember? So instead of landing on the floor, they crashed into something tall and prickly!

'It's a tree!' called Mr Spider. 'I'm pretty sure it's a tree!'

'But it wasn't here last night,' wondered Mrs Spider. 'How did it grow so fast?'

'Perhaps we should explore it,' suggested Mr Spider.

'Excellent!' Mrs Spider agreed. And then, licking her lips, she added, 'I hear that grubs live in trees, and I haven't eaten a grub in a long time!'

So the spiders crawled down the tree. They started from the star at the top. Mr Spider went one way. Mrs Spider went the other. And they were both so excited that they forgot about snipping off the long strands of webbing that trailed behind them.

'Look, here's an orange!' called Mr Spider.

'And an apple!' replied his wife.

There were pine cones and candles and

bows and bells as well—it was a tree full of surprises! But suddenly, just as they reached the bottom, the lights in the room flickered on. So Mr and Mrs Spider did what any sensible spiders would—they skittered far under the tree and into the darkest shadow they could find.

At first, they could see only boots. Big black boots with white fur around the tops. Then there were hands. White-gloved hands thrusting huge bright boxes right in front of their spider faces. Then there was chuckling —and the odd, deep 'Ho-ho-ho'. And finally, from that same deep voice, there boomed a 'What's this?'

The man with the black boots and the white gloves stood back and looked at the tree. And then he laughed again—another 'Ho-ho-ho!'

'A spider's been here,' he chuckled. 'And left its web all up and down and around this tree. It's a lovely decoration. It just needs… yes, that's it.'

And he touched the web with the tip of his white-gloved hand.

All at once, the web turned to silver, from the point where he touched it and all around the tree!

When the man had gone and it was dark again, the spiders crawled out from their hiding place. They looked up at the tree, and at their web, now glistening like silver.

'It's beautiful!' said Mr Spider.

'A wonder!' said Mrs Spider in return.

And some say that's how the very first tinsel came to be!

Francis' Christmas Pageant

The village of Greccio sat on a wooded hill across the valley from Mount Terminillo. On the rocky slopes of that mountain there were caves. And in one of those caves a man named Francis had built a little church.

Francis was a good man, a saint. He rebuilt broken-down churches, helped broken-down people, and travelled across this poor broken-down world talking about the love of God.

One cold Christmas Eve, Francis decided to do something special for the people who lived in Greccio. He called together his friends, a group of monks called the Little Brothers, and he asked them to bring him a wooden manger. He asked for a donkey as well. And a big brown cow. And when he had put them in the cave, he sent out the Little Brothers again.

'Go to the village,' he said. 'Invite everyone. Tell them there is something special waiting for them in the cave.'

The monks did as they were asked and it wasn't long before Francis could see the villagers streaming up the mountainside: a boy with a stick, a little girl, a baker and a blacksmith and a fat old man. A jester and a juggler and a soldier. A tall man on a horse, with a fine lady beside him. A crippled old woman and a beggar and a priest.

They were all there—every one, carrying torches to light their way, so bright against the dark hillside that they could have been stars on that first Christmas night, or the angels who sang to the shepherds.

When they reached the cave, Francis called one woman forward to kneel, like Mary, at the manger's side. Then he asked a man to stand and watch over her, like Joseph. Finally, Francis began to sing. He sang the story of that first Christmas, and the people of Greccio wept when they heard how God had chosen a poor woman, poorer even than themselves, to give birth to his own Son, Jesus.

The story would have ended there, were it not for a monk whose name was John. He had once been a knight—a fierce and powerful warrior. But then he had met Francis and, following his example, he had given up his knighthood and his riches to live in poverty and do good works.

John was there that night too. But as Francis sang the story of Christmas, John alone saw something—something that made him cry out in wonder and joy.

'Look!' he shouted. 'Look in the manger. There's a baby lying there!'

Was it a miracle? Was it a vision sent by God? No one knows. But when the people of Greccio heard that John had seen the Child of Bethlehem lying in that manger, nothing could contain their joy—not the cave, not the valley, not Mount Terminillo itself!

And so they sang God's praises through the night—Saint Francis and the people of Greccio, at the very first Christmas pageant!

Father Joseph's Christmas Song

Father Joseph Mohr trudged through the thick mountain woods. All around him, the world was beautiful. The snow lay like white icing on the branches of the pine trees. And the bright moon above painted the night in shades of winter blue. The young priest, however, missed it all. His thoughts were on other things.

The church organ was broken. There was no time left to mend it. And, worst of all, it was Christmas Eve!

He knew, he just knew, how disappointed the people would be when they came to church the next day to sing their favourite Christmas hymns and carols—only to find that there was no music to accompany them.

But what could he do? Especially now, late at night, as he made his way to bless the birth of a young woodcutter's first child.

Father Joseph shook the snow from his shoulders. Father Joseph stamped the snow from his boots. Father Joseph wished that it were that easy to shake off the problems that troubled him.

But when Father Joseph opened the door of the woodcutter's cottage, he suddenly forgot everything else. For there before him, bathed in the golden light of a blazing fire,

was a picture of the very first Christmas: A young mother, bending over a crib. Her husband, straight and tall behind her. And wrapped in rough blankets, a newborn baby, fast asleep.

Father Joseph blessed the child, and started back home. But he could not forget that picture. He searched for words to describe its quiet beauty. And those words worked themselves into a poem.

When he got home, Father Joseph wrote down that poem. And then, paper in hand, he trudged out into the snow again—to the home of a friend, Franz Gruber.

It was very late by then, but when Franz heard the story and read the words, he knew he had to turn those words into a song. And so, picking the notes out on an old guitar, he composed a tune for Father Joseph's poem.

When Christmas morning arrived, Father Joseph was no longer troubled. Yes, the organ was still broken. And yes, some of the church-folk might well be disappointed. But he was convinced that he had something even better for them—a new song to sing, one that captured the beauty of the first Christmas night.

And so, with his friend Franz Gruber accompanying him on the guitar, Father Joseph sang his Christmas song that day— a song that we sing at Christmas still:

Silent night, holy night,
All is calm, all is bright
Round yon virgin mother and child;
Holy infant so tender and mild,
Sleep in heavenly peace,
Sleep in heavenly peace.

Silent night, holy night,
Shepherds quake at the sight;
Glories stream from heaven afar,
Heavenly hosts sing alleluia;
Christ, the Saviour, is born,
Christ, the Saviour, is born.

Silent night, holy night
Son of God, love's pure light
Radiant beams from thy holy face,
With the dawn of redeeming grace,
Jesus, Lord, at thy birth,
Jesus, Lord, at thy birth.

The Christmas Rose

Abbot Hans loved his garden.

It was his job to run the monastery and care for the monks who lived there. It was a hard job, and it took a lot of patience. So each day, he took a little break and went to the monastery garden where he tended the flowers. Roses and tulips and chrysanthemums —he took care of them all. Planting and watering and weeding. And at his side each day toiled a young monk—Brother Erik, a monk who did not like gardening even one little bit.

'My back hurts!' Brother Erik would moan. 'My knees are all dirty. There's a thorn in my thumb!'

But all Abbot Hans would say was, 'Be patient, Brother Erik. Growing flowers is much like growing men. A little water here. A little pruning there. And then something beautiful blossoms! Learn your lessons in this garden, and you may well be an abbot yourself some day.'

One sunny afternoon a woman passed by.

'What beautiful flowers!' she exclaimed. And before Abbot Hans could thank her for her compliment, she added, 'But I have seen a garden more beautiful still!'

Abbot Hans was curious (and just a little jealous too).

'And where would that garden be?' he asked.

The woman smiled a secret smile. Then she bent over and whispered into the abbot's ear, so that Brother Erik had to strain to hear.

'Every Christmas Eve, near the cave where I live, the forest is bathed in a white light, and it changes into a garden—the most beautiful garden I have ever seen!'

The abbot was more curious than ever. 'You must show me this place,' he begged. 'I would love to see it for myself!'

'Ah, that I cannot do,' said the woman, shaking her head. 'For my husband has been falsely accused of robbery, and that cave is his hiding place.' And with that, she walked away.

Abbot Hans went back to work, but all he could think of was that other garden—that amazing Christmas garden.

'My back hurts!' moaned Brother Erik. 'My knees are stiff. And—look—I have a thorn in my thumb!'

'Then go and join the others,' Abbot Hans muttered, too concerned with that other garden to bother arguing with his young helper.

For a day and a sleepless night Abbot Hans wondered how he might get to see that wonderful garden. Finally, he had an idea. He shared it with the archbishop the very next morning. The archbishop agreed. And the next time the woman passed the monastery, he stopped her.

'I have a plan,' he explained. 'A plan that will help us both, I think. The archbishop has promised me that if I can bring back some proof of this amazing garden—a flower, a root, or a branch—he will speak to the sheriff about your husband and convince him of his innocence!'

The woman stared at Abbot Hans for a moment, and he wasn't sure what she would do. Then she smiled that secret smile again, and nodded.

'Agreed!' she said. 'On Christmas Eve, I will send my son to show you the way.'

Christmas Eve arrived at last, and the woman's son with it. So Abbot Hans and Brother Erik set off on their journey.

'My legs hurt,' moaned Brother Erik, as they walked across a field.

'My feet are killing me!' he groaned as they climbed a little hill.

'Oww!' he cried as they passed a patch of blackberry bushes, 'there's a thorn in my thumb!'

Finally, they reached the cave and, just as the woman had said, it soon became clear that her husband was a kind and honest man. Abbot Hans was eager to see the garden and to admire its beauty, but now he also wanted to help this innocent man!

Day turned into night. The night grew deep and dark. And then, at midnight, the abbot heard the ringing of a little bell.

'That's the signal,' said the woman. 'It happens every year!' So they all walked out of the cave and into the forest.

A great light shone, and where there had been a forest before, deep and white and blanketed with snow, there was suddenly a garden, covered with the purest, whitest roses that Abbot Hans had ever seen.

All was beautiful and peaceful and still, and Abbot Hans exclaimed, 'Have we all been taken to heaven?' Brother Erik, however, was afraid. So afraid that he started to cry out.

'Help me!' he shouted. 'Get me out of here!'

As soon as he'd said it, everything changed. The sky turned dark and a blizzard blew into the forest, so thick and fast that they all lost sight of each other. Everyone stumbled towards the cave but, at the last minute, Abbot Hans remembered his promise to the woman. He had seen the garden, and now he needed to take something back to the archbishop—so that her husband's innocence could be proved.

And so Abbot Hans turned away from the cave and walked into the cold heart of the blizzard. Then he dropped down to his knees and dug around in the freezing snow until he found what he was looking for—a single Christmas rose.

The next morning, Brother Erik found the abbot there—the budding rose between his cold, dead fingers. Gently, he picked up the abbot's body, and carried it back to the monastery. And once the archbishop had seen the rose and once the robber had been pardoned, Brother Erik took the beautiful flower and planted it in the little monastery garden. He tended it faithfully, every day, and he never moaned—no, not once—no matter how hard he had to work.

And that is how the Christmas Rose came from a place near to heaven and into the gardens of ordinary men. And that is also how a young monk, nervous and complaining, learned the patience to become the abbot of a monastery—the best abbot that monastery ever had.

Christmas Tales
and Legends

*Over the years, legends about Christmas—
from the time of the nativity to later
seasonal celebrations—have grown up.
Here are some much-loved stories that
have been handed down from generation
to generation.*

The Raven

Raven was a jealous bird.

He was jealous of Robin and Bluebird and Dove, for they were more beautiful than him.

And he was jealous of Sparrow and Nightingale too, for he could never hope to sing like them.

So Raven flew through the night skies, a sad and bitter shadow, calling out his lonely caw-caw.

One cold December night, Raven sensed suddenly that he was not alone. He felt the sky above him shiver, as if he were in the wake of some much larger bird—Eagle, perhaps, or Vulture. But then Raven heard singing too—singing so lovely that it could never have come from the throats of those two high-flying hunters.

Jealousy struck Raven first. Why should he bother with yet another bird and its golden voice? But curiosity was there as well. And so, fighting his jealousy, Raven looked up into the sky. And there, floating above him, were no birds at all, but a flock of golden angels!

'Good news!' the angels sang. 'We have good news! God's own Son is born in Bethlehem tonight! And you, Raven, must go and tell all the other birds!'

'Me?' Raven croaked. 'Why me? I am the

ugliest of the birds, and as for my voice—well, you can hear for yourselves! They will never listen to me.'

'But you have been chosen,' the angels sang. And, without another word, they flew off into the night.

What could Raven do? The birds had to know. And he, of all birds, had been chosen to tell them. And so he flew down from the sky, down to the tree tops—his cry as sharp and piercing as the winter night.

'Christ is born!' he called—called to Robin and to Bluebird and to Dove. 'Born in Bethlehem tonight!'

'Then we must go and see him,' they chirped. And Raven was surprised, for not one of them mentioned how ugly Raven was.

'Christ is born!' he called again—called to Sparrow and to Nightingale.

'Then we must go and sing to him!' they twittered. And again Raven was surprised, for not one of them said a thing about the harshness of Raven's voice.

And so Raven flew to Bethlehem too. He watched the baby reach out and touch Robin's bright red breast. He heard the baby giggle and coo along with Nightingale's sweet lullaby. And he wished that he could do something more than perch high in the stable's dark rafters.

'But don't you see?' came a voice—a sweet sing-song voice amid the flutter of golden wings. 'You have done the most important thing of all. For none of the other birds would be here, if you had not pierced the night with your cries and told them the good news.'

Then the angel disappeared. And leaving his jealousy behind, Raven took flight too—down from the rafters to join the others at the side of the child.

The Little Lambs

Once upon a time, there were two little lambs. They lived with their flock on a hill outside Bethlehem. And every night, before they fell asleep, they would sit around the fire and listen to the tales of a wise, old shepherd.

Some of the stories were exciting, and the little lambs could hardly get to sleep.

Some tales were funny, and the little lambs would roll with laughter.

Others were scary, and the little lambs would snuggle extra close to their mother sheep.

But one night, the old shepherd told a special tale— a story about something that was yet to happen.

'One day,' he said slowly, 'one day, a king will be born. He will be powerful. He will be good. And he will put right what is wrong in this world. But here is the amazing thing! He will not be born in a palace. He will not be born to the rich and the mighty. No—he will be born to poor and ordinary people. People just like us!'

The two little lambs had never heard such a thing.

'A king!' said the first.

'A king and a shepherd!' said the second.

And secretly, they both wondered the same thing: Where is this king? And when can we go and see him?

One crisp clear night, a few weeks later, the old shepherd told the story again. And when he had finished, one lamb turned to the other.

'I want to see this king!' he whispered.

'Me too!' said the second little lamb. 'Why don't we try to find him—tonight!'

'Yes,' nodded the second. 'When we are looking for grass, we go from hill to hill, don't we? And the shepherd never stops until he finds the greenest pasture. That's what we'll do. We'll never stop, until we find the king!'

And so they searched—from hill to hill and valley to valley, halfway through that dark night. But still they found no baby king.

At last, they came to a road.

'I'm tired,' said the first lamb. 'I want to go home!'

'But here is a road!' said the second lamb. 'Maybe it will take us to the king!'

'You go if you want to,' the first lamb sighed. 'I'm going back.' And that's just what he did.

And so they pretended to go to sleep. They shut their eyes. They baa-ed and they snuffled and they snored. And when their mother sheep was finally fast asleep, they sneaked out of the sheepfold and hurried down the hill.

They peeped into the shepherds' huts first. No baby there.

Then they crept around every dimming campfire. No king there, either.

'What now?' asked the first lamb.

The second lamb thought for a minute. And then he said just one word: 'Grass.'

'Grass?' asked the first lamb.

But the second little lamb would not give up. So he started down that road.

It was dark and it was late and he was frightened. So the little lamb tried hard to remember the old shepherd's funny stories. And he tried even harder to forget the scary ones!

Suddenly, the sky turned bright. Behind him, over the hills, there was light and—could it be?—singing! And ahead of him, the sky seemed brighter too. For a star shone high in the heavens, lighting up a little town below.

The little lamb started to run. Something special was happening, and he wanted to see it, even if it had nothing to do with that special king.

He followed the star to a stable. And there, among the sleepy beasts, were a mother and a father and a baby.

The lamb crept in and nuzzled the child. The child patted the lamb on his woolly head. And it wasn't long before the shepherds, and their sheep—and his tired brother too—came creeping in as well.

'What are you doing here?' asked the old shepherd, when he had spotted the little lamb. 'I know. You're here to see the king I told you about.' Then he pointed at the baby. 'Well, there he is. A good king. A powerful king. A king who will, one day, put right what is wrong with this world. A king born poor and ordinary—just like us!'

The Baby in the Dough

'Add water and flour and knead the dough.'

The baker mumbled to himself as he worked. He liked to hear the words. They kept him company in his kitchen as he baked his bread, loaf after loaf, all day long.

'Add water and flour and knead the dough.'

And then somebody knocked—a frantic Bang, bang, bang! on the baker's door. So he left his dough and wiped his hands and opened the front door.

A man and a woman with a baby in her arms stood frightened before him.

'Please help us!' the man begged. 'My name is Joseph. This is Mary my wife. King Herod's soldiers are looking for us. They want to kill our baby.'

The baker had heard the stories. Babies all around Bethlehem had been killed, because King Herod believed that one of them would grow up to take his throne.

'Come in quickly,' he said. And he bolted the door behind them.

The frightened family huddled in a corner, and the baker went back to his work.

'Add water and flour and knead the dough.'

And then somebody else knocked—a heavy Boom, boom, boom!—on the baker's door. And a gruff voice followed close behind,

'Open up! By order of King Herod!'

'It's the soldiers!' whispered Joseph.

'We're trapped!' Mary whispered back.

But all the baker could think of were those words—the ones that ran through his head, day after day, 'Add water and flour and knead the dough.'

'Of course!' he said, snapping his fingers. It was a strange idea, but it just might work. So he picked up a lump of dough and dumped it in his biggest bowl.

'Give me the baby,' he said, as he hollowed out a place in the middle of the dough. What choice did Mary have? The soldiers were pounding even harder, now! So she handed little Jesus to the baker, and the baker put him in the bowl, pulling the dough right over him, like a big, bready blanket!

'Now, be quiet, little fellow,' he whispered. 'We'll be as quick as we can.'

Then he opened the door and let the soldiers in.

'We're looking for a man, a woman and a baby.' The captain grunted, and he looked suspiciously at Mary and Joseph.

'Well, we have a man and a woman here,' the baker said, 'two of my best customers, in fact. But I don't see any baby!'

The captain grunted again, and then led his soldiers in a search of the baker's house. They looked in cupboards and chests and emptied out every bucket and pot and drawer. But they paid no attention at all to the big bowl of dough that sat on the table, right in front of them!

At last, the soldiers left. And as soon as they did, the baker pulled back the dough. There was baby Jesus— a little sticky, perhaps—but otherwise unharmed!

'Thank you,' said Joseph.

'You've saved us all!' added Mary.

Then, later that day, when the soldiers were long gone, the little family left as well.

And the baker? His day finished just as it

had started. In his kitchen. With his pots and pans. Adding water and flour and kneading the dough.

The Greedy Woman

Mary and Joseph and little Jesus were on their way to Egypt.

They yawned. Their tummies growled. And even though King Herod's soldiers were looking for them, they knew that they had to rest.

A little town lay ahead of them. And so Mary and Joseph decided to stop there for the night. It was already late when they arrived, and there were lights in the windows of only two houses.

The first house was enormous!

And when Mary and Joseph knocked at the door, they were met by an equally enormous woman!

'What do you want?' she grunted. She was dressed in great finery. In fact, she was the richest woman in town.

'A place to stay for the night,' Joseph answered.

'And a bite to eat,' added Mary.

The rich woman looked them up and down. They were dirty from their journey, and little Jesus was starting to make a fuss.

'Well, there's no room here!' she said gruffly. Then she slammed the door in their faces.

'It's just like in Bethlehem,' sighed Mary.

'Yes,' Joseph nodded. And then he forced a little smile. 'But who knows?' he added, 'Perhaps the next house has a stable!'

As it happened, the next house did not have a stable. In fact, it was hardly bigger than a stable itself! It was a tiny, run-down little place. And when Mary and Joseph knocked at the door, they were met by an equally tiny woman!

'How can I help you?' she asked.

'We need a place to stay,' said Joseph.

'And perhaps a bite to eat,' Mary added.

'Well, come in then!' said the little woman, with a smile.

The little house was almost empty—except for a table and a chair and a spinning wheel.

'My husband is dead,' the little woman explained, 'and so I must spin yarn, day and night, to make a living.'

Mary and Joseph felt sorry for the woman, but she would not let them leave. She fed them, and let them sleep on her best blankets.

In the morning, Mary turned to her and said, 'We have no way to repay your kindness—no way but this: make a wish this morning. Any wish you like. And I promise you that your wish will come true!'

The little woman looked puzzled. She had never heard anything like this before. But she smiled and said goodbye, and when her visitors had gone, she returned to her spinning.

She worked long. And she worked hard. And in the middle of the morning she sighed and said to herself, 'I wish, I truly wish, that I could spin much finer yarn. For then I would not have to work so hard.'

And as soon as she wished it, it was so. The yarn that ran through her fingers turned at once into the most beautiful yarn she had ever seen!

She spun all that day and through the night, and it wasn't long before that beautiful yarn made her a very rich woman indeed!

Everyone was happy for her. Everyone, that is, but the enormous woman in the enormous house—the richest (and the greediest!) woman in town. She begged and she nagged and she pleaded with the little woman to tell her the secret of her beautiful yarn. And finally, one day, the little woman gave in and told her the story of her three late-night visitors.

The greedy woman couldn't believe it. She was angry at the little woman for her luck, and even angrier at herself for having missed the chance to get richer still. And so she vowed that she would help those three visitors if she ever happened to meet them again.

One day her chance did come.

King Herod had died, and it was now safe for Mary and Joseph and little Jesus to return home. On their way back to Nazareth, they passed through the same little town.

The greedy woman was at the well, filling a clay jug with water, and when she saw the visitors, she set it on the ground beside her.

'How nice to see you again!' she cried. 'You must be tired. You must be hungry. Come to my house, rest and eat!'

'No, thank you,' said Joseph, politely. 'It's still the middle of the day, and we have a long way to go until we can take the time to rest.'

'Please!' the woman begged. And here she looked at Mary. 'Or at least grant me a wish for having been kind enough to offer.'

Mary looked back at the woman and sighed. 'Very well, then. Make a wish—any wish. And I promise you that your wish will come true.'

The big woman jumped up and down. She clapped her hands together. And she ran home in such a hurry that she left her water jug behind.

What shall I wish for? she wondered. What would make me the happiest? A thousand gold coins? Marriage to some prince? A kingdom of my own, perhaps? And as she thought, she began to get thirsty, so she started to make herself a cup of tea.

But when she went for the water, there was none to be found.

So, without thinking, she said, 'I wish I'd brought that jug with me.'

And as soon as she'd said it, the water jug came flying through her window!

And that was the end of that greedy woman's wishing.

The King of Christmas

King Christopher sighed and sat down on his throne. It was time to choose a new chief counsellor.

Just then, Lord Percy, Lord Pickle and Lord Punch—the three main candidates—burst into the room.

'Greetings, Your Majesty!' they said, each trying to bow lower than the other. And then the arguments began.

'I have the most money!' boasted Lord Percy.

'I am the wisest!' bragged Lord Punch.

'But I am connected to the most important families!' announced Lord Pickle.

And it went on like that, for hours.

When the lords finally left, the king was exhausted—and no closer to making his decision.

'Your Majesty,' came a voice from the corner of the room. 'May I make a suggestion?'

It was Jumble, the court jester.

'Of course,' the king sighed, 'as long as there's a joke to go with it.'

The jester grinned, 'I suppose you could say that a joke is exactly what I had in mind!' Then he half-whispered, half-chuckled his idea to the king.

The next day, King Christopher summoned the three lords.

'You will agree,' he said, 'that the chief counsellor needs to know the king's mind— what the king would do in any situation, how the king would act.'

'Yes, Your Majesty,' they bowed.

'Well then, here is your task. I intend to play a part in this year's royal Christmas pageant. All the actors, myself included, will be wearing masks.

'Whoever guesses which part I am playing will become my new chief counsellor. But the losers will have to give up both their lands and their titles!'

This was not what the three lords had expected. But their pride would not let them back down. So they bowed and said together, 'As you wish, Your Majesty.'

When Christmas Eve came, the palace air was thick with the rich scents of roasted boar, mulled wine and plum pudding. Bells and trumpets announced the start of the pageant, and the three proud lords were led to their seats on the very first row.

The story of the first Christmas was played out before them, and when it was finished, the three lords clapped louder than anyone. Then Jumble the jester jumped on to the stage and asked the three lords to join him.

'Fine ladies! Noble gentlemen!' he announced. 'This is a special night indeed. For not only is it Christmas Eve, but also the night on which our king will choose his new chief counsellor!'

The audience applauded politely, and the three lords tried to look as important as possible.

'The next chief counsellor,' the jester continued, 'will be the man who is able to pick the king out from our little cast of Christmas characters. Lord Percy, you may choose first.'

Lord Percy straightened his shoulders and held his head high.

'To anyone accustomed to riches—as I am—it is plain that our king has chosen to play a wealthy man. Yes, His Majesty is one of the three kings—the king who brought the GOLD!'

Lord Pickle sneered. 'A foolish choice, if I may say so.'

'And you may!' announced the jester. 'For you are next!'

Lord Pickle examined the cast. He thought deeply. 'Our king is, indeed, a wealthy man,' he said, 'but he is also a wise man. And what is wiser than the wisest of men? An angel, of course! So I say that our king has played the part of the angel Gabriel!'

The crowd seemed pleased with this choice. Some of them even clapped. But Lord Punch quickly interrupted them.

'No!' he announced. 'You have missed the point entirely. Who is the most important man in this story? Not the king. Not even the angel. No, it is the one with the best connections—the man chosen to be the earthly father of Jesus. I say that the king has played the part of Joseph!'

Once again, the crowd applauded, but Jumble held up his hands to silence them.

'Ladies and gentlemen,' he said (with a chuckle in his voice), 'there is only one way for us to know which of these noble men has won the day.'

And with that, he walked over to the Three Kings and removed the mask from the one who held the gold.

The crowd laughed out loud, and Lord Percy groaned. For under the mask was Henry, the butcher's son!

Next, the jester removed the mask from the angel Gabriel.

Lord Pickle cringed. The crowd laughed louder still. For it was Bertha, the royal maid!

Lord Punch grinned smugly, and walked over to Joseph.

'I am delighted to serve Your Majesty,' he said. And he bowed before the carpenter Joseph.

'Ah yes,' the jester sniggered. 'Now that you no longer have lands and titles, Punch, you may indeed need to seek work from this man.' And he pulled off the mask.

'Look!' he announced. 'It's Toothless Bill, the rubbish collector!'

Lord Punch gasped. The crowd roared with laughter. And the jester beamed at the success of his joke.

'This is a trick!' Lord Percy fumed. 'If the king has not played the parts we have chosen, then I say that he is not here at all!'

'Not so,' the jester answered calmly. 'The king has been on stage almost since the play began.' And with that he pulled the head off… the donkey!

The crowd went silent. And Lord Punch began to shout.

'This is an outrage! The king—a donkey? It's treason, I say!'

'Calm down, Punch,' the king commanded. 'You still don't understand, do you? The King of Heaven himself came to be born among the poor. What greater honour then, for a king like myself, than to play the part of the beast who humbly carried that Child and his mother?'

The king shook his head. 'Sadly,' he admitted. 'I did not always see myself that way. I was proud like the three of you. And so I have chosen as my next chief counsellor the man who suggested I play this part—and who showed me the humility a true king should have.'

Then he raised his hand, and laid it on the shoulder of Jumble the jester!

The crowd stood and cheered. The three lords hung their sorry heads.

And the jester and his lord looked at the baby in the rough wooden crib and gave thanks for the true King of Christmas.

Brother Comgall's Christmas

Christmas was coming and Brother Comgall should have been happy. He should have been hanging decorations. He should have been planning games. He should have been making preparations for the Christmas feast that he shared with the boys in his monastery each year.

He should have been excited and filled with joy. But he wasn't. For a great famine had struck Ireland and there was almost nothing left to eat.

A little mouse crept up the side of Brother Comgall's chair, then hopped onto his desk. But Brother Comgall did not chase the mouse away. Instead, he smiled weakly and said, 'Hello, my friend.' And from his pocket he pulled a tiny bit of bread, and an even tinier piece of cheese.

The mouse began to chatter and squeak.

'What's that?' asked Brother Comgall. 'Oh, I see. You will not have any unless I eat some too? Yes, you are right. We have always shared our meals together. But there is so little, my friend. Hardly enough for you, let alone for me!'

The little mouse, however, would not be persuaded. He chattered and squeaked his protest until Brother Comgall finally broke off a bit for himself as well.

The 'meal' took hardly any time at all. And when they had finished, the mouse began to chatter again.

'Yes,' Brother Comgall nodded. 'I thought of that too. The Prince of Ulster has food to spare. But his storehouse is full because he has stolen that food from every family in his charge. He is an evil man, my friend, and I cannot believe that he would help us.'

But the mouse would not give up. He twitched his nose. He chattered and squeaked again. And Brother Comgall smiled.

'No,' he said at last. 'I suppose there would be no harm in asking.'

And with that, he said farewell to his little friend, bundled up in his warmest robe, and set off for the castle of the Prince of Ulster.

Outside it was bitterly cold. Ice hung from the trees. Snow was piled knee-deep. And the wind howled so loudly that Brother Comgall could hardly hear himself as he hummed a Christmas hymn.

Inside the castle, however, everything was warm. And as Brother Comgall entered and bowed, he found the prince and all his friends sitting behind a long table—piled high with meat and bread and pies.

'What do you want, monk?' barked the prince through a mouthful of food.

'Something to eat,' Brother Comgall answered. 'Not for myself, but for the boys —the sons of your own people whom we teach to read and write.'

'Why come to me?' the prince asked. 'You teach that your Christian god takes care of you. Why not beg from him?'

'Because you have food to spare,' Brother Comgall continued, 'but the boys have nothing.'

'The boys would be of more use to me if you taught them how to use a sword!' the prince growled. And then he rose to his feet. 'What do I need with men who can read and write? Teach them how to kill, and then they will be worth feeding!'

Brother Comgall could stand this no longer.

'I will do no such thing!' he answered. 'I will teach them to read and to think—and to know the difference between goodness and greed. And perhaps, one day, this land will have a leader who knows how to care for his people!'

'Throw him out!' the prince ordered. So the guards grabbed Brother Comgall and threw him to the ground, outside the castle gates.

He was bruised when he got up, and bleeding too. And as Brother Comgall hobbled home, the pain in his head and legs grew worse and worse, until he collapsed in the snow in front of the monastery door. Fortunately, one of the other monks spotted him, carried him into the monastery and tucked him into bed.

Brother Comgall slept for the next three days, his body wet with the sweat of a hot fever. There were times when the other monks thought that he might never wake again. But on Christmas morning, as they huddled around his bed in prayer, Brother Comgall opened his eyes.

'What day is it?' he asked, weakly.

'Christmas Day,' they answered.

'Then what are you doing here?' he asked. 'You should be bringing the food from our storehouse and preparing the great Christmas feast!'

The monks looked at one another, worried. Perhaps the fall had rattled Brother Comgall's brains!

'But the storehouse is nearly empty!' one of the monks explained. 'Surely you remember the famine!'

'Of course I remember,' said Brother Comgall. 'But as I lay here, fighting the fever, I was praying.' And then he chuckled. 'It was the Prince of Ulster's idea, actually! And I believe that God has answered my prayers. So, go! And bring what you find.'

The monks went. And when they opened the storehouse doors, they could not believe what they saw. The room was full! Full of meat and bread and pies. So full that there was enough for the boys in the monastery that Christmas Day, and for all their families too. It was the best Christmas feast any of them could remember!

Late that night, the little mouse came to

visit Brother Comgall. He crept onto the bed and scampered across the covers. As always, the monk had cheese and bread waiting for him.

'Where have you been?' he asked. 'I've missed you these last few days.'

The little mouse chattered and squeaked. And when he had finished his story, all Brother Comgall could do was shake his head in wonder.

'Have I got this right?' he said. 'One of your cousins was under the Prince's table? He heard what the Prince said to me? He saw what the Prince did to me? And so he called you and a thousand of your other cousins, and in the middle of the night, you took every bit of food from the Prince's storehouse and carried it here to the monastery?'

The little mouse nodded his head. He squeaked and he squealed and if Brother Comgall hadn't known better, he would have sworn that his little friend was giggling!

'Thank you,' said the monk. Then he bowed his head and thanked God too—for a miracle more amazing than he could ever have imagined.

And the monk and the mouse ate their little Christmas meal together.

Papa Panov's Visitors

It was Christmas Eve.

The lights danced merrily in the streets. Families laughed and sang and unwrapped their presents.

But Papa Panov, the village shoemaker, sat in his home, alone.

His wife was dead, his children grown up and moved away. And so he sat by himself, an old Bible in his lap, and looked for company in the story of the first Christmas.

There were Mary and Joseph, tired and hungry, with nowhere to stay.

I would have given them a room, Papa Panov thought. There is plenty of space in this old house of mine.

There were the shepherds too. And the angels. And three kings from the East bearing gifts.

'Now what would I have brought?' Papa Panov wondered. And he reached for a little box, perched on the top of the highest shelf in his shop. There were two tiny shoes in that box, sewn once upon a time by his own nimble fingers—fingers now grown gnarled and stiff.

'That's what I would have brought him,' Papa Panov smiled. 'My very best work!' Then his head dropped slowly to one side, his glasses fell crooked across his nose, and Papa Panov fell fast asleep.

All Christmas Eve he slept. And while he slept, he dreamed. He dreamed of his wife and of his children and of the happy Christmases they had shared. He saw their faces, just as he remembered them—laughing and singing and shining with joy. And just as the aching sadness of that dream became too much for him to bear, Papa Panov saw another face—a kind and gentle face.

'I am Jesus,' said the face. 'I have seen your loneliness and your sorrow. And so, this Christmas Day, I shall visit you. Watch for me, Papa Panov!'

The old man woke with a start. The morning sun was shining in his eyes. It was Christmas Day! And if the dream was true, then Jesus was coming to visit him!

Papa Panov tidied up his house. He put a pot of fresh coffee on the stove. And then, every few minutes, he peeped out of the window. And that's when he saw the man.

It could have been Jesus, walking slowly down the street, holding a shepherd's staff. But as the man got closer, Papa Panov recognized him. It was Sergei, the village street sweeper, faithfully doing his job, even on Christmas Day.

Papa Panov opened his door and called to the man. 'You look cold, my friend. And it must be lonely out there on Christmas morning. Come in and join me for a cup of coffee!'

The street sweeper hurried into Papa Panov's house. He dusted the snow from his shoulders. He rubbed his freezing hands together. And when Papa Panov handed him the hot mug, he just held it for a while and let the steam rise like a warm cloud over his cold face.

Sergei drank his coffee slowly and, though Papa Panov chatted politely with him (and even told him about the dream!), the shoemaker still kept an eye on the street outside.

'Well, I hope your dream comes true,' said the street sweeper, at last. 'But I have to get back to work. Thank you for your coffee and your kindness.' And with a grateful 'Merry Christmas!' he picked up his broom and went back to sweep the street.

One hour passed. Then two. And slowly, the street became busy. Papa Panov put on a pot

of cabbage soup and watched his neighbours wander off to visit their relatives. But still there was no sign of Jesus.

There was a girl, however. A girl he did not recognize. She walked slowly along the street —a bundle in her arms. And because her clothes were torn and ragged, she shivered with each step.

Papa Panov opened his door again. He looked up and down the street, and when he was sure that Jesus was not there, he called to the girl, 'Come here! Come in from the cold!'

Papa Panov poured out another cup of coffee, and gave the girl a seat close to the stove. He offered to take her bundle, but the girl clutched it tightly to her chest. And that's when the bundle began to cry.

'My baby's hungry,' the girl whispered. So Papa Panov warmed some milk. And as the girl fed the baby and slowly unwrapped the thin blankets, Papa Panov noticed that the child had no shoes.

His thoughts flew straightaway to that little box again. The one perched on the top of his highest shelf.

'But those shoes were for Jesus!' he argued silently with himself.

The baby cried again, and another look at those frozen toes settled the argument once and for all. Papa Panov reached up, took the box down from the shelf, and put the little shoes before the girl.

'I can't take those,' she wept. 'They are far too fine for someone like me.'

'For the child's sake then,' Papa Panov pleaded. 'For Christmas.'

When the girl had gone, Papa Panov looked out of the window again. The sun was low in the sky now, and there was still no sign of Jesus. But there were plenty of beggars, wandering the streets in search of a little Christmas cheer. So Papa Panov opened his door to them. He had a pot of cabbage soup after all. And they slurped it down gratefully.

It was dark by the time the last beggar left, and Papa Panov was tired. So he slumped down in his chair again, more sad and lonely than he had been the night before.

'It must have been a dream.' He sighed. 'Only a dream.' And at that moment, Papa Panov knew that he was not alone. He looked up, and there was that face again. It was Jesus, standing in the doorway.

'When I was hungry,' Jesus said, 'you fed me. When I was cold, you comforted me. And when I was naked, you gave me something to wear.'

'But when?' asked Papa Panov. 'When did I do these things for you?'

'When you warmed the street sweeper, and fed the beggars, and gave your finest shoes to a poor and shivering child. That's when,' Jesus smiled.

'Merry Christmas, Papa Panov,' he said at last. Then he disappeared into the night. Like a vision. Like a ghost. Like a dream.

Christina's Christmas Garden

Christina and her mother lived in the forest. Their home was a cave. Their beds were made of straw. They ate stew made of berries and wild onions. And they wore clothes made of animal skins.

The people in the village nearby made fun of Christina and her mother—not so much because they were poor, but because they were different!

The only villager who was kind to them, in fact, was the old priest, Father Robert.

'You are very special!' he would often say to Christina (for he could tell those kinds of things), 'One day, God will use you to do something amazing!'

One Christmas Eve, when both forest and village were blanketed with snow, Christina walked to the church. She had to pass through the village to get there, and was amazed at what she saw through every window: people sitting before warm fires, laden plates of food and brightly decorated trees—more beautiful than any in the forest —with children dancing around them

'If only my home,' she wished, 'was as beautiful as one of these!'

And so she pushed her face up against every window. She licked her lips and she stared. But every time the villagers caught sight of her, they chased her away, and the children stopped their games for a moment to call her names as she ran off into the snow.

By the time she reached the church it was nearly midnight. Christina was freezing and frustrated and sad, but not nearly as frustrated as old Father Robert.

'It's the church bell,' he explained. 'I need to ring it—to welcome in Christmas. But the rope is frozen solid and it won't budge.'

'Let me try to fix it!' offered Christina.

And before Father Robert could say, 'That's all right' or 'How?' or anything at all, she had started to climb the tall tower.

'Be careful!' the old priest called. But Christina was not the least bit frightened, for she had climbed trees twice that tall.

When Christina reached the top, she started to rock the bell. She tugged on the frozen rope, as well. And, little by little, it began to move. There was just a gentle Clink-clank at first, as the clapper tapped against the bell. But the harder she tugged the rope, the louder the bell rang—until the Clink-clank grew into a Ding-dong and then into a noisy BONG-BONG!

Father Robert waved thank you as the

villagers ran into the streets to wish each other a Merry Christmas.

And then something happened that no one expected.

Maybe it had to do with the coming of Christmas. Maybe it had to do with the ringing of the bell. Or maybe it had to do with Christina's wish—her wish that her own home might be decorated as beautifully as the homes of the villagers. But as the bell rang, the forest where she lived did, indeed, begin to change. The snow began to melt. The trees blossomed with buds. Flowers shot up out of the ground. Small animals climbed out of their burrows. And the forest was made lovely with the sights and smells of spring! Christina's home was no longer a cold and wintry place, but a beautiful Christmas garden.

As the villagers looked around in wonder and Father Robert said a prayer, Christina climbed down from the tower. And as she ran to find her mother, flowers burst into bloom wherever her little feet touched the ground!

When she had gone, the villagers went back to their homes. And when they woke up the next morning, winter had returned and everything was as it had always been. Except for one thing—everyone realized that Christina was not only different, but special. So they never made fun of her or her mother again.

The Little Fir Tree

'I wish I weren't so little,' the little fir tree moaned.

The baby bunnies hid under his branches. The children danced around him and sang. But he never enjoyed their company—not for one minute. For all he could do was stare up at the tall pine trees and long for the day when he would be tall too.

Time passed. The little fir tree grew. But still he moaned.

'I wish I was one of those really big trees,' he complained to a sparrow one day.

'Why?' asked the sparrow. 'The squirrels play in your branches. The children have picnics in your shade. Why not be happy with what you are?'

'Because those tall trees must be happier still!' the little fir tree sighed. 'They are so close to the sky and to the sun. And more than that, a stork once told me that when they are chopped down, the tall trees are turned into masts for ships and that they spend their lives sailing across the seas! Oh, how wonderful to be a tall tree,' the little fir tree sighed again.

'Well, I'm no stork,' the sparrow twittered. 'But I have seen wonderful things too! Why, just last winter, I perched on the window sill

of a beautiful house in the town. And inside that house, I saw a tree—not much bigger than you—decorated with candles and ribbons and apples and toys!'

'Not much bigger than me?' the fir tree repeated.

'Exactly!' chirped the sparrow. 'So be happy with what you are!' And then the sparrow flew away.

From that moment on, the fir tree could think of nothing but the sparrow's story. He ignored the bright hot summer and the crisp autumn breeze. He forgot about the squirrels and the children too. For all he could do was dream about that beautiful tree, and wish for winter to come.

Come it did—with cold and snow and ice. And with it came the men, as well, with axes slung over their shoulders. When they saw the little fir tree, one of them shouted, 'Here's the one!' and then with a few well-placed blows they chopped the fir tree down.

The axe hurt the little fir tree. But for once, he did not moan. All he could think of was how beautiful he soon would be.

The man with the axe carried the fir tree to a very smart house. And soon the little fir tree's dream came true. He was propped up in the corner of a huge room, and then covered with ribbons and candles and toys— just as the sparrow had said!

That evening, the candles were lit, and even though they singed the fir tree's branches, still he did not complain, for as soon as the children looked at him they clapped and cheered. They were happy. And at long last, he was happy too. His happiness, however, lasted only for a minute. For as soon as the children had finished cheering, they gathered around the tree and stripped his branches of the ribbons and toys and fruit!

'Oh dear!' the fir tree sighed. And then he calmed himself with this thought. 'Perhaps they will decorate me again tomorrow!'

The next day came. There were no more decorations. And none the day after, or the day after that. In fact, no one paid him any notice at all. And when a few more days had passed, an old servant picked him up and tossed him onto a pile of rubbish behind the house. The fir tree's branches were brittle now, his needles dropping off.

'I wish I was back in the forest,' he moaned.

'Oh, it's not so bad here,' said a little rat. 'There's plenty of rubbish to eat! You should be happy with where you are!'

'I was happy once!' the little fir tree remembered (though he did not remember very well!). 'I lived out in the woods with the squirrels in my branches and the children at my feet.' But before he could remember another thing, the servant returned and set fire to the rubbish pile—and the little fir tree as well.

The rat scampered away. A sparrow flew overhead. And the tree's sap spluttered and fizzled a sad moaning sound.

'I wish I were…' the little tree whispered. And then the little tree said no more.

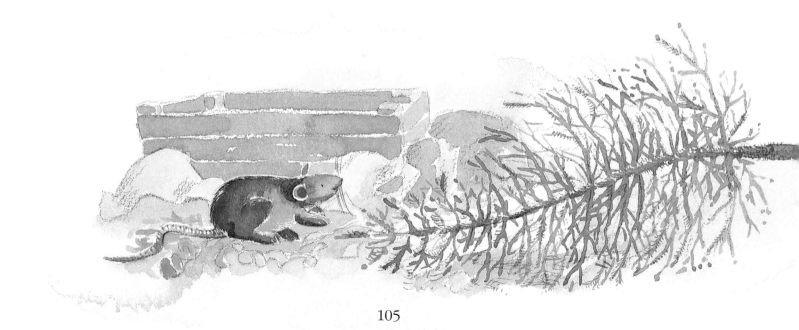

The Four Seasons

It was Christmas Eve, the very coldest day of the year, and little Marushka sat sobbing and shivering in the corner. Her stepsister, Holena, and her stepmother did not like her. They called her names and made her do all the hard housework. And why? Simply because Marushka was beautiful—and they were jealous of her.

'Marushka!' came the harsh voice of her stepmother. 'Marushka, come here at once!'

Marushka dried her eyes on her apron and walked slowly into the next room.

'Hurry up, girl!' her stepmother snapped. 'Your stepsister, Holena, would like some fresh violets for Christmas. Go into the woods, at once, and fetch them for her.'

'But, stepmother,' Marushka said quietly, 'It is winter time. There are no violets in the woods.'

'Then you must walk until you find some,' Holena sneered, from her comfortable chair on the other side of the room.

'Now go!' the stepmother ordered. 'Or I will give you a beating you will never forget!'

Marushka nodded and said nothing more. She wrapped herself up in the warmest clothes she could find and set off through the deep snow to look for a bunch of fresh violets.

She walked and she walked and she walked, weeping with every step.

'I will freeze to death out here,' she wept (which was exactly what her stepmother and stepsister had planned), when suddenly she saw a light, burning bright at the top of a little hill. So she hurried there, as fast as her frozen feet would carry her.

When she arrived, she found twelve men sitting silently around a fire. Three were very old. Three were a little younger. Three were younger still. And the last three were no older than boys. Marushka did not know it, of course, but these were the Twelve Months of the Year!

'What do you want?' asked the oldest of them all.

'I-I've c-come to pick violets,' Marushka shivered.

'But this is my month, December,' said the old man. 'There are no violets in the forest now.'

'I-I know,' answered Marushka, shivering harder still. 'But my stepmother says she will beat me if I do not return with them.'

'I see,' said the old man. 'Then we must do something about that. Brother March,' he called, 'come, take my place.'

One of the younger men stood up and traded places with old December. And soon, everything began to change.

The snow melted. A robin redbreast appeared. And buds sprang out from the bare tree branches. Suddenly, it was spring! 'There are violets aplenty now,' said Brother March. 'Pick them quickly and take them to your family.'

Marushka thanked the man, scooped up a bunch of violets, and hurried back home.

Her stepmother and stepsister were surprised to see her. But they were even more surprised when she reached into her coat and pulled out the violets.

'But… how? And where did you find them?' asked Holena.

'In the forest. Up on the little hill,' said Marushka, matter-of-factly. Then she went straight to bed.

The next morning, Marushka's stepmother shook her awake.

'Get up, you lazy girl!' she shouted. 'Your stepsister, Holena, would like a bowlful of strawberries for her Christmas breakfast. You must go into the woods and find some.'

'But it's winter!' cried Marushka. 'There are no strawberries…'

'Do as I say!' her stepmother shouted again. 'Or I will give you a beating you will never forget!'

So once again, Marushka bundled herself up and trudged out into the snow. This time she headed straight for the little hill. The Twelve Months were still there, sitting around their fire.

'What do you want this time?' asked old December.

'Strawberries,' answered Marushka, more than a little embarrassed. 'For my stepsister.'

'And if you do not return with them?' asked December.

'Then it's a beating I will never forget.'

'I see,' December nodded. 'Brother June, come, take my place.'

Soon it was summer on the top of that little hill. So Marushka filled her apron with sweet fresh strawberries.

'Thank you again,' she said to the men.

And she hurried back home.

'I don't believe it!' cried Holena, when Marushka had returned. But it did not take her long to gobble down every berry.

'Apples!' she shouted, the strawberry juice still dripping from her greedy lips. 'I want apples, now! Go, fetch me some.'

'But it's winter,' Marushka tried to explain. 'And there are no apples.'

'No apples?' grinned Holena. 'Don't tell me that. I'm sure there are plenty of apples up on that little hill of yours. As a matter of fact, I'm sure there are plenty of good things up there you have never told us about. You want to keep them for yourself, don't you? Well, we'll see about that.'

And before Marushka or her stepmother could stop her, Holena burst out the door and rushed off into the woods. She raced through the snow, hardly thinking about the cold, until she came, at last, to the place where the Twelve Months sat.

'What do you want?' asked December, exactly as he had asked Marushka.

'Mind your own business, old man!' snapped Holena. 'I'm looking for apples. My stepsister Marushka has already brought me violets and strawberries, so I am sure there are apples out here too.'

December frowned. He did not like this rude girl, nor the way she spoke of her sister. So he raised his ancient arms, and the fiercest of December winds began to blow. A blinding snowstorm followed, so Holena wandered about, lost in the blizzard and the cold.

When she did not return that night, her mother wandered out into the snow in search of her. And she, too, was never seen again.

As for Marushka, she had never wanted to go out into the snow in the first place. So she built up a warm fire, moved from her corner to a place in front of the hearth, and had her merriest Christmas ever!

The Cobbler's Sons

The cobbler said goodbye to his three sons, then trudged down the mountainside to the village below.

It was Christmas Eve—a bad time to leave the boys alone. But there were soldiers in the village, home from the war. And the cobbler hoped that mending the soldiers' boots might help fill his empty cupboards and the bare place under the tree where the presents should have been.

'Do not let anyone in. No matter what they say,' he warned the boys. And they nodded their heads as they had done so many times before.

Once their father had gone, the boys tucked themselves into their one wide bed. There was nothing to eat after all. And no new toys to play with. So they hoped that in their dreams, at least, they might have a happy Christmas.

However, that was not to be. For as they tried to fall asleep, the wind began to blow. The tree branches scratched against the windows and the wooden shutters clapped like hands against the walls.

Frightened, the boys pulled the blanket right up to their noses. And that's when they heard the knock!

'It was the shutters,' said the middle brother.

'It was the trees!' said the youngest.

'It was a knock,' said the oldest brother. 'I'm sure of it!' And he climbed out of bed and peeped out the window to see who was there.

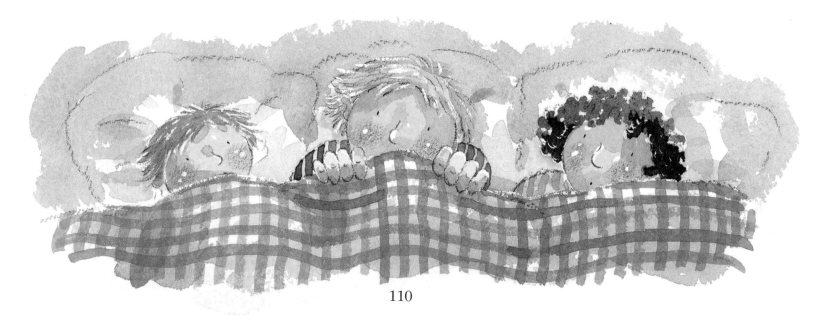

110

'It's a man. A little man,' he said, 'with pointy ears and a big bulb of a nose. It looks as if he's freezing!'

'Don't let him in!' cried the middle brother.

'Remember what Papa said,' added the youngest.

But again the oldest brother was sure of himself. Maybe too sure!

'I can't let him freeze!' he said, 'Not on Christmas Eve!' And he opened the door and let the stranger in!

'What kept you?' the little man shouted. 'Didn't you see me freezing out there? Where's the hot cocoa? The warm fire? The steaming bowl of soup? This is no way to treat a guest!'

The two youngest brothers looked at one another, puzzled. The man did not seem grateful at all!

'But we have no fire,' the oldest brother explained. 'And no food, either.'

'Gobbled it down already?' the little man shouted. 'Greedy boys! Well, the least you could do is to make a little room for me in your nice warm bed.'

As it happens, it wasn't a nice bed, at all. For the mattress was lumpy and the blanket was thin. But the little man didn't seem to notice. He leaped into the bed between the two younger brothers and grabbed up half the blanket!

'Wait just a minute!' the oldest brother said.

Soon, he was doing cartwheels as well. But it was buns and cakes and cookies that spilled out of his pockets!

Then the little man looked at the youngest brother, who was hanging on to the tiniest corner of the blanket.

'Still too cold!' he shouted, but as he kicked the smallest boy out, the other two brothers cried, 'No! He doesn't know how to do cartwheels!'

'You'd better turn him upside down and shake him, then!' the little man grunted.

And so they did. And all three of them laughed when gold and silver coins poured out of his pockets!

But when he tried to climb back into bed, the little man kicked him out! The oldest brother went spinning across the room. And when he hit the floor, the spinning didn't stop. Instead, he started doing cartwheels, right around the room.

He couldn't help himself, and he was about to cry for help, when he noticed that fresh oranges and chocolates and other sweets came tumbling out of his pockets, every time he turned upside down!

Meanwhile, the little man kept tugging at the blanket.

'Still not warm enough,' he grumbled. And he kicked out the middle brother too!

The floor was covered now—with cakes and sweets and coins. But when the boys turned to thank the strange little man, he was gone!

It wasn't long before their father returned home, his arms full of food and presents he'd bought with his boot-mending money. He thought his boys would be surprised. But it was the cobbler who was shocked instead.

'Where did all this come from?' he asked. And when the boys had told him the story—shouting and laughing and interrupting one another—the cobbler grinned. He was so surprised, in fact, that he even forgot to tell them off for letting a stranger into the house.

'Your visitor was old Laurin,' he explained. 'King of all the goblins! The legends say that he visits one home, every Christmas. He plays his tricks. He leaves his gifts. Then he disappears into the night. I always thought it was make-believe.' Then he looked at the treasures all over his floor. 'But now I know it's true!'

Together, they scooped up the candy and the money and the cakes. And the cobbler and his sons had their best Christmas ever!

The Little Juggler

Up and down and round and round, the yellow balls danced high into the sky.

In the summer, there had been cheering crowds and coins in the little juggler's cup. But now that winter had arrived, no one wanted to stand outside and watch. And so the little juggler was cold and hungry and poor.

Up and down and round and round, he leaped and tumbled and rolled—just to keep himself warm. And when he had no strength left even for that, he sat down in the village square and began to cry.

'What's the matter, my child?' asked a kindly old monk.

The little juggler dried his eyes. 'I have no mother or father,' he sniffled. 'No money, no food, and no place to stay!'

The monk looked at the little juggler. He was just a boy—no more than nine or ten.

'I have an idea,' said the monk. 'Why don't you come to the abbey with me! It's a little draughty, I'll admit, but there is plenty to eat and drink. And besides, I have always thought that we could use a juggler around the place!'

And so the little juggler went with the monk to the abbey. He had food and drink and a place to stay. And, best of all, he had an audience!

Up and down and round and round, the little juggler danced and somersaulted and juggled for the monks. And, just like the crowds in the market, they clapped and cheered and called for more.

As Christmas drew closer, however, the monks seemed less interested in the little juggler's tricks.

'We have much to do,' the old monk explained. 'Each of us must make a Christmas gift for the baby Jesus and his mother Mary.'

Up and down and round and round, the little juggler wandered about the abbey, watching the monks. Some painted pictures.

Some composed songs. Some wrote out scriptures in the most beautiful handwriting. And some carved wooden screens to place around the altar.

I wish I could make something beautiful, the little juggler thought, something special for the Virgin Mary and her child.

Christmas Eve arrived at last, and the monks paraded into the chapel, where the statue of the Virgin Mary stood. They placed their gifts before her, and the little juggler watched with tears in his eyes, for he had nothing to bring. But as the monks paraded back out again, the little juggler had an idea. He lingered behind in the shadows and, when the monks had gone, he stood alone before the statue.

'Dear Lady,' he said, 'I have nothing beautiful to bring. But I can juggle. And so my juggling is what I will give to you this Christmas Eve.'

Up and down and round and round, the little juggler leaped and rolled and tumbled before the statue. But what he did not know was that there was someone else watching too—his friend, the kindly old monk. He had gone to the juggler's room to wish him a good night and had found the boy missing.

The old monk didn't know what to do. He had never heard of anyone juggling in a chapel. He didn't even know if it was right. But what he did know was that the boy's juggling and tumbling was better than he had ever seen it. And so he just stood there in the darkness and watched.

When the little juggler had finished, he collapsed, exhausted, on the floor of the chapel and fell fast asleep. The old monk stepped forward to pick up his little friend and carry him to his room. But before he could take a second step, he had a most amazing vision! He watched in wonder as the Virgin Mary herself—no longer a statue— walked down from behind the altar, accompanied by a host of angels.

Up and down and round and round the angels flew, filling the chapel with their songs. And while they sang, the Virgin Mary cradled the little juggler in her arms and thanked him for his Christmas gift.

Then as quickly as they had come, the Virgin Mary and the angels were gone. The old monk rushed into the chapel. 'It's a miracle!' he cried. And soon the whole abbey was awakened by the news.

'You brought the best gift of all!' said the monk to the little juggler. 'Because you gave the very best you had to give.'

And so the little juggler juggled before the altar again—up and down and round and round—that day, and the next, and every day for the rest of his long and happy life!

A Note from the Author

Many of the stories in this book are retellings
of traditional tales from around the world.
They have been retold by many people over
the years and I am just the next in a long line
of storytellers. Each of us uses slightly different
words and phrases, and so the stories evolve.
You may wish to read other versions of some
of these stories, so I would like to acknowledge
some of the sources I have referred to, although
most of these stories can be found in several
collections. You will find the stories listed under
the titles used in this book, but they should be
easy to identify in the books I mention.

'The Four Seasons' from *Favorite Fairy Tales Told in
Czechoslovakia* by Virginia Haviland, Beech Tree Books,
1995. 'The Littlest Camel', 'The First Tinsel', 'The Raven',
'The Baby in the Dough' and 'The Greedy Woman' from
Hark! A Christmas Sampler by Jane Yolen, G.P. Putnam'
Sons, New York, 1991. 'Old Befana', 'Kind Bishop Nicholas',
'Wenceslas' Winter Walk', 'A Flower for Christmas', 'The First
Christmas Tree', 'The Icicles', 'Francis' Christmas Pageant',
'Father Joseph's Christmas Song' and 'The Christmas Rose'
from *It's Time for Christmas* by Elizabeth Hough Sechrist
and Janette Woolsey, Macrae Smith Company, Philadelphia,
1959. 'Brother Froilan's Carvings', 'The Little Lambs' and
'Brother Comgall's Christmas' from *Joy to the World* by
Ruth Sawyer, Little, Brown and Company, Boston, 1966.
'The Little Juggler' from *The Little Juggler* by Barbara Cooney,
Hastings House, New York, 1961. 'Papa Panov' from *The
Lion Christmas Book* compiled by Mary Batchelor, Lion
Publishing, Oxford, 1984. 'The Cobbler's Sons' from *The
Remarkable Christmas of the Cobbler's Sons* by Ruth
Sawyer, Viking, New York, 1994. 'Christina's Christmas
Garden' from *Tales to Tell Around the World* by Pleasant
DeSpain, August House Publishers, Little Rock, 1995. 'The
Little Fir Tree' adapted from a tale by Hans Christian Andersen.